Contents

Acknowledgements

The author and publishers wish to thank the following who have kindly given permission for the use of copyright material:

Associated Book Publishers for an extract from *Economic Structure and Policy* edited by T. Barker and published by Chapman Hall Limited, 1976;

Associated Newspapers Group Ltd. for an extract 'The Best of British' from the *Daily Mail* 12.10.78;

The Controller of Her Majesty's Stationery Office for data from *United Kingdom Balance of Payments 1964-74;*

The Daily Telegraph Limited for a report 'Nice Timing by Treasury' in the issue of 3.11.78;

J.M. Dent & Sons Limited for an extract from *The Principles of Political Economy and Taxation* by D. Ricardo (Everyman's Library Series);

The Financial Times Business Information Limited for extracts in *The Financial Times* issues of 2.3.78 and 8.6.78;

Guardian Newspapers Limited for an extract from the article 'A strong pound that may prove a weak link' in the *Guardian* 5.7.79;

London Express News and Feature Services for the article 'Why flagging exports could ruin the Government's Promised Land' in the *Sun* 17.2.78;

Longman Group Limited for an extract from *The Farm Business* by Norman and Coote (1971);

Marine Midland Bank N.A. for figures from the Daily Market Report;

Norman McCord for an extract from his book *Free Trade;*

Syndication International Limited for an extract from the *Daily Mirror* 'Comment' column in the issue of 10.2.78;

Times Newspapers Limited for extracts from articles in *The Sunday Times* 'Trade in Potatoes' 30.4.78, 'The pound holds steady up to June' 5.6.77, 'One man's bid to buy British' 21.5.78, 'Why the buck will stop here' 29.10.78, and from *The Times* an extract from a report 'Exporting Rail' 12.5.78, and the leader 'Bad for New Zealand' 13.6.78.

Every effort has been made to trace all the copyright holders but if any have been inadvertently overlooked the publishers will be pleased to make the necessary arrangement at the first opportunity.

Casebooks on Economic Principles

~~INTERNATIONAL~~

London and Basingstoke

LIBREX

First published 1983
Reprinted 1983

Published by
MACMILLAN EDUCATION LIMITED
Houndmills Basingstoke Hampshire RG21 2XS
and London
Associated companies throughout the world

Printed in Hong Kong

British Library Cataloguing in Publication Data

Leake, Andrew
International economics. — (Casebooks on
economic principles).
1. Commerce
2. Finance
I. Title II. Series
382 HF91

ISBN 0-333-27992-1

Casebooks on Economic Principles

INTERNATIONAL ECONOMICS

Andrew Leake
Head of Economics
Latymer Upper School, Hammersmith

Macmillan Education
London and Basingstoke

First published 1983
Reprinted 1983

Published by
MACMILLAN EDUCATION LIMITED
Houndmills Basingstoke Hampshire RG21 2XS
and London
Associated companies throughout the world

Printed in Hong Kong

British Library Cataloguing in Publication Data

Leake, Andrew
International economics. — (Casebooks on
economic principles).
1. Commerce
2. Finance
I. Title II. Series
382 HF91

ISBN 0-333-27992-1

1 Introduction

Theory and practice

Learning to drive a car is not easy. You may read all the books, be told what to do by your instructor, and still not be able to do it all by yourself. It takes theory and practice together.

So it is with economics. The theory explains in general terms what should be happening. It takes all possibilities into account. It can be learned from teachers or from textbooks.

For most of us, however, the appeal of economics lies in the practical side of the subject. Just as we want to be able to drive a car for ourselves, so we want to be able to consider and understand the economic problems we see in the real world. It is the purpose of this, and the other Casebooks, to consider theory and practice, side by side.

Stage by stage

You have to do many different things to drive a car. You have to control the steering, the accelerator, the brakes and the gears. Although you will use them all together in the end, it helps if you can try them one at a time at the start.

It is the same with economic theory. We need to understand many different ideas, and the connections between them. By taking ideas one at a time, from each area of the subject in turn, we will eventually have built up a complete picture.

So it is the approach in this, and the other Casebooks, to study each important principle in a separate section, and to consider economics stage by stage.

How to use this Casebook

Each section considers a particular aspect of economic behaviour. It does this in three ways. First there is a brief outline of the general principles involved. Next there is an illustration of the way those principles apply in the real world. Finally there are questions based on the issues raised in the section, and arising from the material studied.

The outline of theory is a concise summary of work that has already been covered. It does not develop the general theory to any great depth, but restates and reinforces the most important aspects of each economic principle. It aims to provide a complete preparation for all that follows in the section, and in the rest of the Casebook.

The applications are of individual principles, rather than of broad topics. Their use will be in making practical sense of abstract ideas, and in providing examples to illustrate theoretical points. They are the sort of decisions that are made by individuals and governments each day: things that matter to all of us.

It is hoped that this material will be of interest both for its economic content and in its own right.

International Economics

We will study a variety of very different types of questions in this Casebook. Questions of *trade* will be to do with the process of exchange between countries, or any other trading partners: why is it there, and is it good or bad? Questions of *payments* will be to do with the monetary system which supports that exchange: what sets the level of payments, and how will they affect a country? Questions of *exchange rates* will be to do with the relative value of each country's currency: what sets the exchange rate, and what effect does it have on trade and other things?

These questions tend, in the main, to follow from those that are studied in other areas of economics. In this Casebook, therefore, we will start from the assumption that the reader is already familiar with the analysis of markets, and national income. We will use the terms 'supply', 'demand', 'leakages' and 'injections' to answer many of the questions that arise.

2 The theory of trade

2.1 Trade and exchange

The theory of trade deals with the exchange of goods and services. This is a large topic, and in one respect none could be larger. For the complete story of exchange will include every department of microeconomics, beginning with the productivity of factors of production, and ending with the final consumption of goods and services. It is only possible to understand the theory of trade in its entirety, therefore, when one already understands the behaviour of markets, and the decision-making of producers and consumers, in some detail.

So, let us summarise the interaction of the different areas of microeconomics, as part of the free market system. This will provide a basis for the particular arguments on trade that follow later.

The market system

We begin with an increase in consumer preferences towards a particular good. This will cause an increase in market demand for that good, at each price level (as shown by the theory of demand). In the short term, before supply can respond, the market clearing process will encourage a rise in the equilibrium price of the good. This change in relative price will attract producers into the market (as explained by the theory of supply), and the higher price they offer for factors of production will change patterns of employment (as in the theory of factor markets). In the long term, therefore, there will be a redistribution of factors away from alternative work and into production of the good whose relative price has risen. The increased output of these factors results in a move along the long-term supply curve of the good, and a supply of goods to meet the new pattern of consumers' tastes.

In this way, the market system ensures that the pattern of consumers' tastes will set the allocation of factors of production between different employments.

If exchange is limited to a domestic level only, then the tastes of a country's own consumers will determine its use of factors. If trade is then offered at an international level there will be a new way of using factors, to meet the international pattern of consumers' tastes.

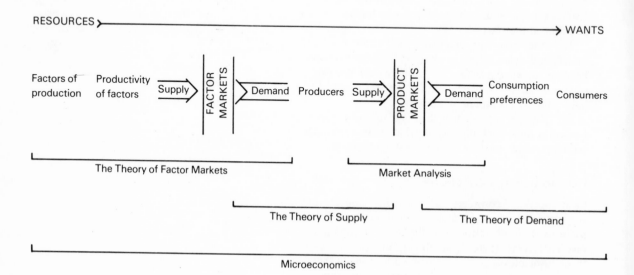

The market system

6

2.2 Positive or normative?

'What Britain and Japan sell to each other'

The trade between Britain and Japan raises two quite different economic issues. On the one hand there is the question of the range and quantity of goods and services traded between Britain and Japan. Is there an explanation for the pattern of this trade? The search for an objective explanation will be an exercise in *positive* economics.

On the other hand there are the advantages and disadvantages of this trade from Britain's point of view. This will involve us in value judgements on what is 'good' or 'bad' for the country, and provide an exercise in *normative* economics.

The explanation of trade patterns between Japan and Britain is unlikely to be a simple one. Goods such as Scotch whisky and diamonds may be imported by Japan because she produces none of her own, but most of the goods mentioned (cars, radios, machinery, etc.) could be produced by either country.

The arguments for and against trade are important because the gains to the British consumer, in being able to choose the cars and TV sets that he prefers, seem to be offset by losses to the British manufacturer. The British motor-cycle industry has already fallen victim to Japanese competition, and many others seem to be similarly threatened.

Economists are interested in both issues, and try to study them separately, even though this may prove difficult. The gains from trade, for instance, provide the motivation for trade to continue and are thus part of the explanation for it.

Both exercises carry implications for government policy. The explanation of the trading process, and the causes of the overall pattern of trade between countries, will present the government with information on how best to implement any policy they decide on. The arguments in favour of trade in general, but for protection from foreign competition in particular cases, will make them decide what their policy should be. A government would be poorly prepared for decision-making if only one approach were to be adopted at the expense of the other; each has a valuable role to play.

What Britain and Japan sell to each other

Britain and Japan have been trading with one another for the past hundred years, and today the level of exchanges has reached the £1,000 million a year level.
. . .

The kinds of goods which our two countries sell to each other are remarkably similar. The things which Britain buys from Japan are very varied, with transport equipment (which largely means cars and motorcycles), electrical machinery (including radios, TV sets and tape recorders) and steel being the largest single components. These days it seems to be common for people in Britain to regard these imports from Japan, especially in the categories of cars, electronics and steel, as having an adverse effect on the British economy.

Cars and TV sets, of course, are supplied only to consumers who deliberately choose them out of the range of models available to them. Steel products are used in many ways, but it is interesting that one of the reasons for the increase in imports from Japan in 1975 was the heavy demand for seamless steel pipes for main piping use, a valued technological innovation of Japan's highly specialized steel industry which has proved of vital importance to the fast development of North Sea oil production. Japanese exports have thus helped indirectly but substantially to enlarge Britain's future economic stake in this new asset.

Britain's exports to Japan are equally various, with beverages (especially whisky), textiles (especially woollen cloth) and machinery of all kinds (notably aero-engines and tractors) high in the list. Platinum, diamonds and pharmaceuticals are also strong selling lines.

QUESTIONS

Which of the following propositions are (a) positive, (b) normative?

(i) Imports of cars, electronics and steel from Japan are bad for Britain.

(ii) Imports of cars, electronics and steel from Japan have an adverse effect on the British balance of payments.

(iii) The import of seamless steel pipes allowed development of North Sea oil to proceed more quickly.

(iv) Britain should not need to rely upon Japan to develop North Sea oil.

(v) Britain and Japan can both increase their consumption of goods by trading with one another.

3 Explaining trade

3.1 The causes of trade

'One man's bid to buy British'

Britain imports tea from India, radios from Japan, shirts from Macao, and McDonald restaurants from the USA. These are all examples of international trade, but they are examples of different *types* of international trade, since each is explained by different economic principles. It will be useful to distinguish between five different causes of international trade.

(i) *Trade to get goods and services that are otherwise unavailable*

One boy has only peashooters, and another has only a bag of dried peas. They can obtain both types of good only by 'swapping', and through this trade both boys will become better off.

At an international level, this situation will arise when one country has an extreme advantage over others in production of a good. For instance, natural resources are only found in certain areas, and high technology products may be available from only one country. Countries that are physically incapable of producing such goods will have to trade if they are to consume them at all.

Britain imports many products that fall within this category, rather than any other. Besides tea from India, Britain will also need to import the 'raw material for milk bottle tops' or go without.

(ii) *Trade due to a comparative advantage in production*

This is a more complicated situation. Suppose that one girl is better at maths homework, and the other is better at physics. They *could* each do both subjects, but if they prefer to specialise in only one, in order to 'swap' their answers, they may get better results overall. It is still possible to gain from this specialisation even if one girl is better at both subjects than the other, providing each is better, by her own standards, at a different subject.

In a similar way, countries can specialise in those goods and services in which they have a comparative advantage in production, and trade to the benefit of

One man's bid to buy British

The Prime Minister has called on the nation to "buy British, make British and sell British." Will Ellsworth-Jones discovered just how easy it is to let imports creep into your life.

At eight o'clock, the Japanese alarm goes off. I turn on the Japanese radio, slide out of bed on to the Indian rug, put on my British slippers and go downstairs to make a cup of Marks and Spencer's Indian tea, packed in a British teabag.

Turn on a very efficient British kettle, open the German fridge and get out the milk (courtesy of the good old British cow, bottle made in Britain, foil top made in Britain from raw material mined in central America). Pour the boiled British water into a British cup, add Mauritian sugar (refined in Britain) and stir with a Japanese spoon.

Back to an antique British bed, to read by British newspaper printed on Canadian or Scandinavian newsprint. Shave with razor (blade and soap all British). Dab on American aftershave. Clean teeth in an all-British operation.

Like one man in three in Britain, I put on Marks and Spencer's British underwear and socks, a British shirt, American trousers and jacket and a pair of shoes from Ireland.

My daughter puts me to shame – she is moved out of her British nappie, into an entirely British outfit. Mothercare says that 98.9 per cent of its goods are British-made. Its labels proclaim the products are "carefully made in Great Britain," as though the rest of the world are making them carelessly.

Put some British (Sainsbury's) cereal from a British package into a Japanese bowl on an antique British table. Give up the struggle with the American toaster and use the grill on the British cooker. Spread New Zealand butter on to brown bread (a mixture of American, Canadian, French and British wheats) and enjoy a cup of Kenyan coffee.

Grab an umbrella – origin unknown, but since it cost only £2 off an Oxford Street barrow, I suspect it fell off a Japanese lorry. Catch a British underground train to Oxford Circus. Up a British-made escalator and use a French-made photo-copying machine in the station.

all. Although Britain is capable of producing its own radios, and shoes, it finds it cheaper to import large quantities of those goods from countries that specialise in their production, such as Japan and Italy. In effect the previous principle is simply an extreme case of differences in production advantages such as these.

In Oxford Street, it is clear that at the cheap end of the market for items like shoes or shirts, British goods cannot compete with those made in the low-wage places such as Korea and Hong Kong.

Some sales assistants say there is still quite a lot of "Buy British" feeling among customers but admit they can't always satisfy the demand.

Start at a shoe shop where a rack on the pavement contains shoes from Italy, India, Portugal and Spain. Not one British shoe. On to British Home Stores. Amid the sports shirt section, all my worries about the pound come flooding back; the labels say Hong Kong, Korea, Taiwan and Macao.

One sports shirt (£3.99) does carry a British label. An identical shirt, at an identical price, carries a Macao label. The store explains that it is not simply a question of price. The fact is that the British manufacturer simply cannot supply the required quantity quick enough.

On to a McDonald quick-service restaurant for lunch. Roll, hamburger and sauce from England, pickles and onion from America. Container is British, paper bag German.

Bob Rhea, McDonald's managing director, says the company had great trouble in finding a British manufacturer prepared to invest in the machinery needed to fold napkins in the McDonald way.

I learn that every European eating a McDonald apple pie is eating a British-made apple pie.

Back to Oxford Street, fighting my way through the tourists who make it possible for us to afford all our imported goodies.

Into John Lewis for a glass of British milk. My money goes into a Swedish cash register.

Then, a meander through the domestic appliances, where the old fears surface again. Out of 13 dish-washers on display, only one — a particularly small one — is British. The Norwegian salesgirl laments the fact that she has no other British products to sell to the steady flow of customers who, she says, still ask if they can buy British.

End the shopping expedition by trying to buy a floppy cricket hat. The only one I can find comes from Hong Kong and doesn't fit.

Back home to drown all my guilt feelings about the imports I possess . . . in a French glass of Spanish wine.

(iii)   *Trade due to differences in tastes*

The two previous causes of trade have concentrated on production differences. Now we must consider differences in consumption tastes. Two boys each have the same selection of sweets, but one boy prefers one type of sweet, and the other prefers a different type. Again, they can 'swap' to their mutual benefit.

In the real world it can be very difficult to see this principle at work, on its own. It will most often coincide with a difference in production conditions as well, so that the two causes of trade either oppose, or complement one another. For instance, it might be arguable that Britain has a higher demand for umbrellas than Japan has (or than most other countries have?), *and* that Japan has a comparative advantage in their production. Both influences would encourage a trade of umbrellas from Japan to Britain.

If, however, Britain and Macao have the same comparative production costs for sports shirts, then any imports from Macao would probably be due to the greater comparative demand shown in Britain.

(iv)   *Trade in factors of production*

Exchange does not take place only in terms of the output of factors of production, but in terms of factors of production, such as labour and capital, themselves. One of the main differences between trade within a country and trade between countries is over the question of how much this will happen. Factors of production can usually transfer between different jobs much more easily within a country than between countries.

McDonald quick-service restaurants are the product of an American company. Although much of their service in Britain involves the employment of British factors of production, the first steps in production will have involved some transfer of factors from America to Britain. The management to organise the business, and funds to hire British factors of production, will probably have been traded themselves.

(v)   *Trade for other reasons*

The trade described so far has all been justified by sound, commercial reasons. A surprising amount of trade in the real world cannot be explained entirely in this way, since it is based heavily on cultural, historical or political ties. The pattern of this type of trade is one that economic theory cannot hope to predict and that falls outside our area of interest.

QUESTIONS

From the extract 'One man's bid to buy British', find one example, not quoted above, of each of the following types of trade:

(i)   Trade in a good that cannot be produced in Britain

(ii)   Trade due to comparative advantage in production

(iii)   Trade due to differences in tastes

(iv)   Trade in factors of production.

3.2 Comparative advantage

Of the five causes of trade, we will concentrate here upon the theory of comparative advantage alone. To make matters clear, it is helpful to explain how trade can proceed between two countries producing only the same two goods. We will assume that none of the other influences upon trade has any part in this explanation. Here trade is caused by differences in the relative costs of production alone.

What is a comparative advantage in production?

It will take a double comparison to find out which of two countries has a relative advantage in producing which of two goods. The first half of the comparison is in terms of the relative costs of producing each good. The second half is in terms of the differences between countries.

The cost of producing each good will depend upon the particular conditions of its supply. With scarce resources, a country will only be able to produce more of one good by producing less of the other. The rate at which it can exchange its production of them will set the comparative costs of making each good.

If comparative costs are different in each country, there is a comparative advantage in production — each good can be exchanged more cheaply in one country than in the other.

How can comparative advantage be measured?

The comparative costs of producing two goods can be expressed in two ways. The first is in terms of the *quantity of resources* needed to produce one unit of each good. Whether measured in man-years, acres of land or whatever, the fewer resources that are needed, the lower are the relative costs of production.

A second way to express the same idea is in terms of *production possibilities*. Producers could choose to use all of their resources to produce one good, or the other. These options can be shown as extreme cases, or, in terms of a whole range of alternatives, as a production possibilities frontier. In each case, the amount of one good that must be given up to produce more of the other will measure comparative costs, and be found from the slope of the production possibilities line.

'Oats or barley?'

Farmers have to choose what to produce from their limited supply of land, knowing that they will have to

Oats or barley?

Comparative advantage or comparative costs

This economic principle explains the reason why any economic unit, whether a farm, county or region, concentrates on the production of those items for which its relative advantage is the greatest (or its relative disadvantage is least). It is the basic reason why arable cropping predominates in the East of England and grass production is common in the West. The principle can be simply explained by reference to two farms both in the same area each growing 200 acres of cereals in their cropping programme, but because of different soil types the following average levels of cereal yields are obtained:

	Farm A per acre	Farm B per acre
Oats	2.0 tons	1.25 tons
Barley	1.75 tons	1.5 tons

From these average yield figures it can be seen that Farm A has a comparative advantage in favour of oats (the land will yield more oats per acre than barley). Farm B has a comparative advantage in favour of barley (the land will yield more barley per acre than oats). The tendency therefore will be for Farmer A to specialise in oat growing and for Farmer B to grow barley. The fact that Farmer A has an absolute advantage over Farmer B in growing both oats and barley (i.e. the yields are higher than on Farm B) does not affect the principle of comparative advantage.

In deciding whether or not to specialise, both farmers would reason along the following lines — Farmer A must sacrifice ($\frac{2.0}{1.75}$ = 1.14) tons of oats if he wants one ton of barley (because the oats on his farm yield 2.0 tons per acre, but the barley only yields 1.75 tons per acre). Farmer B, on the other hand, must sacrifice ($\frac{1.5}{1.25}$ = 1.2) tons of barley, if he wants one ton of oats. It follows, therefore, that it will be to each farmer's advantage to specialise, especially if Farmer A can acquire a ton of barley for less than 1.14 ton of oats, and if Farmer B can acquire a ton of oats for less than 1.2 ton of barley.

produce less of one crop if they are to produce more of another. The different conditions of supply in different parts of the country will mean that the quantity of one crop they can exchange in production for another will vary from place to place.

Consider, for instance, the case of two farms producing only oats and barley. Farm A has measured its comparative costs of production and found that it can produce barley more cheaply than oats. Farm B has done the same and can produce oats more cheaply than barley. In the comparison between them there is a clear advantage in production to Farm A in barley and to Farm B in oats. Although comparative

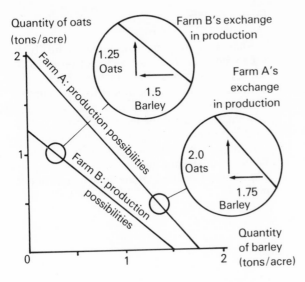

Quantity of oats (tons/acre)

Farm B's exchange in production

1.25 Oats
1.5 Barley

Farm A's exchange in production

2.0 Oats
1.75 Barley

Farm A: production possibilities

Farm B: production possibilities

Quantity of barley (tons/acre)

Diagram 1   Oats or barley: production possibilities

costs have been measured in terms of extreme production possibilities, by assuming that oats and barley can be produced in constant proportion, and in suitable combinations, these possibilities can be shown on a diagram (1). The double comparison drawn between products and between producers identifies a clear comparative advantage in production for each of these farms. The same approach can be applied to countries, and establish a basis for trade between them.

A basis for trade

All other things being equal, a difference in the comparative costs of producing two goods between two countries will provide a basis for specialisation, and trade. Production differences will make each good appear more scarce in one country than in the other, and if this scarcity is reflected in relative prices, there will be an incentive to produce goods for trade. We will study the way this trade proceeds in a later section.

There are, however, a great number of other things that can influence this result. One is that production possibilities themselves will change, if factors of production transfer between trading partners, or are altered in any way. Another is that production possibilities may not always change in equal proportion. Diseconomies of scale will make it more difficult to expand output by concentrating resources in the production of one good, but economies of scale will make it easier. Either situation will change the conditions of supply from those we have described so far.

QUESTIONS

(i)   Express the production possibilities of Farms A and B, in oats and barley, in terms of a table of the number of acres needed to produce one ton of each crop.
(ii)   Assume that the production possibilities of Farm A change so that it can now produce three tons of barley per acre, but all other figures stay the same. Is there any comparative advantage now, and if so, in which good for each farm?
(iii)   Redraw diagram 1 to express these new production possibilities.
(iv)   Suggest two changes in the conditions of production which might enable two farms in the same area to alter their relative production possibilities.

What causes differences in comparative costs?

One farm may have a production advantage over another because of differences in the type of soil on which they work. One country may have an advantage over another for a similar, but more general, reason. Each good can be made at lowest cost only by employing particular types and amounts of factors of production. Each country has a different endowment of factors which it can use in production. Countries can, therefore, produce goods at different comparative cost, and make best use of all their resources through specialisation, and trade.

'Lancashire cotton'

Cotton manufacture used to be one of the major industries in Britain. Lancashire could claim, with pride, a clear comparative advantage in production over the rest of the world. The threat of foreign competition could be dismissed as 'twaddle', so strong was the basis for that advantage. The cotton manufacturers believed that they had an advantage in producing cotton goods for three reasons:
(i) Lancashire labour was different from foreign labour, in that it was more skilful in spinning and weaving. Furthermore, foreigners could 'never find the brains Lancashire cotton men have for the job'!
(ii) Factors employed in Lancashire were capable of producing more cotton than in other parts of the world, because Lancashire had 'got the only climate in the world where cotton piece goods in any quantity can ever be produced'.
(iii) Lancashire had much more capital equipment with which to produce cotton goods: there were 'more spindles in Oldham than in all the rest of the world put together'.

Lancashire cotton

I recall another day in 1911. I then realised for the first time what it meant to commit sacrilege. Innocently I noted the growth of spindles in Japan, and the sharply dwindling British trade in cottons with Japan. Rashly I commented aloud on it in the presence of a manufacturer. He gave me an angry lecture about the iniquity of the tariffs to which Japan had taken. Then the majesty of Lancashire's unchallengeable greatness came upon him again, and he finished serenely: 'My lad, never again let anybody in Lancashire hear you talk this childish stuff about foreign competition. It's right enough for Londoners and such like, but it puts a born Lancashire man to shame as an ignoramus. It's just twaddle. In the first place, we've got the only climate in the world where cotton piece goods in any quantity can ever be produced. In the second place, no foreign Johnnies can ever be bred that can spin and weave like Lancashire lasses and lads. In the third place, there are more spindles in Oldham than in all the rest of the world put together. And last of all, if they had the climate and the men and the spindles — which they never can have — foreigners could never find the brains Lancashire cotton men have for the job. We've been making all the world's cotton cloth that matters for more years than I can tell, and we always shall.'

QUESTIONS

Assume that the arguments used to justify Lancashire's production advantage in cotton in 1911 were correct at the time. Explain how this comparative advantage might have been lost to Japan since 1911, by showing what production changes might have arisen under each of the three headings:
(i) different types of factors in different countries;
(ii) different production possibilities from the same factors in different countries;
(iii) different amounts of the same factors in different markets.

These three advantages can be expanded from the particular case of Lancashire cotton to a general view of what it is that causes comparative cost differences. The three general causes will be, therefore:
(i) countries possess different types of factors of production,
(ii) factors are capable of producing different amounts of a certain good in different countries,
(iii) countries possess different amounts of each factor.

In its original form, the theory of comparative advantage relied upon differences in labour as being the most important cause. Now we can give the other factors their appropriate weight, and predict that all factors will affect a country's comparative production costs, as with Lancashire cotton.

With all three types of production advantage to support him, is it any wonder that our cotton manufacturer could claim, 'We've been making all the world's cotton cloth that matters for more years than I can tell, and we always shall'?

Unfortunately, he has been proved wrong. Other countries have developed the factors of production with which to compete with Lancashire, and comparative advantage has moved significantly against this industry in Britain.

3.3 The trading process

Trade between countries does not happen 'by luck', any more than trade between areas, or people. Neither does it require a central authority to order or control events, for it happens automatically, through the work of the market system, once the right conditions exist.

The conditions for trade

Dealers buy in one market in order to sell in another, if they find that they can make a gain by doing so. This incentive will be the same, whatever the separation between markets, providing that the same type of good is sold in each. The motivation will be lost, however, if there are costs in trading which outweigh the gains.

For example, ticket 'touts' are dealers at a local level, trading tickets from one market, or part of a market, to another. They buy in the official market, well in advance, and sell in a 'black' market, when tickets are more scarce. Their activity is typical of the work of all traders, in several respects. . . .

They only enter the business if it offers them an opportunity to gain personally, from a difference between buying and selling prices. They do not want tickets for their own use, but buy only in order to resell. They carry on their trade unless they are discouraged by trading costs or restrictions (such as prosecution by the police!).

Why do prices differ?

Price is set by supply and demand, which measure the use of resources, and the strength of wants, respectively. When all is working well, therefore, the market system will ensure that price reflects scarcity.

If supply and demand set price at a low level in one part of a market, such as the official advance sales of tickets, but at a high level in another part of the market, such as the last-minute black market for tickets, then this will reflect a difference in relative scarcity. Trade between the markets will tend to balance scarcity, and price, as shown in diagram 1.

Differences in prices at an international level will also, all being well, reflect scarcity. If wants are the same in each country, then price levels will depend on the resources used to produce goods. Prices will be set by costs, and comparative advantages in production will lead to the prices of goods being different between countries. Those price differences will motivate dealers to begin trading goods.

The effects of trade

As the process of trade begins to affect a country, both its production and consumption change. Dealers will be buying more of any good in which the country has a comparative advantage, and is, therefore, producing relatively cheaply. Their increased demand will tend to raise the price of the good, at the same time as encouraging an increase in produc-

Stage 1: price lower in one market than in another. Dealers buy there (shifting demand in that market), then sell at the high price (shifting supply in the other market). This continues until at *Stage 2* price is the same in both markets.

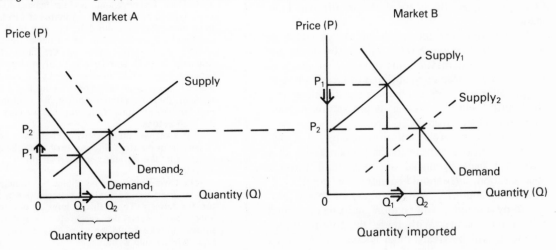

Diagram 1   Trading between two markets selling the same good

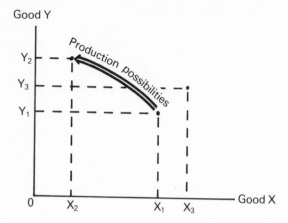

Good Y

Y_2 · · Production possibilities

Y_3

Y_1

0   X_2 X_1 X_3 ——— Good X

Before trade: production of X = X_1, of Y = Y_1
and consumption = home production.

(Assumes a comparative advantage in production of
Good Y, and production under diseconomies of scale.)

With specialisation: production of X falls to X_2,
of Y rises to Y_2.

(Assumes that trading conditions and demand patterns
are suitable.)

With trade: consumption of both X and Y rises,
to X_3 and Y_3.

Diagram 2   The effects of trade on production and consumption in a country

tion. Both these effects are shown on diagram 1, in
market A.

By contrast, the increased imports of goods in
which other countries have a comparative advantage
will encourage domestic firms to reduce production,
in the face of cheap competition. Producers will tend
to specialise according to comparative advantage, and
the country will move along its production possibilities frontier (see diagram 2).

Consumption levels will also change. Through
trade a country's consumers can obtain goods that
have not been produced at home, and through
specialisation, there should be more of all goods available to all countries. Without trade, all that is produced by a country, and no more, must be consumed
within the country. With trade, the country's consumption will be greater than is allowed for by its
own production possibilities. Dealers may gain most
directly from these new opportunities, but all producers and consumers will be able to gain as well.

'Trade in potatoes'

We are concerned here with a time when the market
price of potatoes in Britain shot up from £53 a ton
at the end of March to £80 a ton at the end of April.
In the main, this rise was the result of government
intervention which, with hindsight, seems to have
been excessive. Whatever its causes, it was not
matched by changes on the continent, and so gave
Holland a significant price advantage in the sale of
potatoes.

As we would expect, the difference in prices
encouraged a trade in potatoes from Holland to
Britain, and it was in order to protect British farmers
from this competition that the government imposed
an import ban. The restriction did not apply to
'processed' potatoes, however, and in the market for
frozen chips the international trading process could
proceed normally. (In fact we are told that 'enter-

Trade in potatoes

If you shopped at the green-grocers yesterday, you
may have noticed that the price of potatoes is shoot-
ing up rapidly and wondered why this should be
when there is supposed to be a big surplus of potatoes.
The beady-eyed will also have noticed that frozen
chips are cheap and not going up.

The answer, as if you had not guessed, is that the
Government has been doing its best to help. And if
you think you're annoyed at paying more, then British
chip firms, potato merchants and Dutch farmers are
furious.

For, with the best of intentions, the Ministry of
Agriculture, Fisheries and Food has managed to create
a shortage of potatoes, cost the taxpayer £16m, throw
small chipmakers on the dole, create a black market
and find itself challenged in the European Court.

The story starts down on the farm. The dry
summers of 1975 and 1976 cut our potato crop and
brought high prices in the shops. So the farmers
planted as much as they could. After last year's wet
summer, they harvested a bumper five million tons of
potatoes against trade estimates that we only needed
3.7 million tons.

For a change, the housewife should have been able
to get cheap potatoes. Indeed, they were cheap – too
cheap for the farmers as market prices tumbled
alarmingly.

The Government had no choice but to help out. It
is committed to a guaranteed average price of £48 per
ton for farmers. To do this, it buys up potatoes. But
how many? After the years of shortage and high
prices, no one could be sure how many potatoes
housewives would want.

Doing its sums as best it could, the Ministry bought

prising traders' were still trading in the main potato market as well, despite the legal restriction.) The trade affected the prices, production and consumption of chips, in the way predicted by our theory.

The price of frozen chips fell well below the price of potatoes, due to the increased supply from Dutch imports. The production of frozen chips in Britain fell markedly, in the face of this foreign competition, and firms laid off workers or closed down. If the situation had persisted into the longer term, firms would even have begun to move into new areas of business, in line with the change in relative prices. British consumers, on the other hand, were gaining the benefits of trade in cheap and plentiful chips!

In this example, the trading process worked quickly as dealers took advantage of a change in relative prices. That change was caused only by a temporary imperfection in the market system, in the form of government policy, but nevertheless it influenced the pattern of trade. Similarly any other change in prices will influence trade, whatever its cause.

If comparative costs set relative prices exactly and exclusively, then any trade that follows will be explained by the principle of comparative advantage. If, however, prices are affected by other influences, of which differences in demand and market imperfections are the most important, then comparative advantage will offer only a part of the explanation of trade.

QUESTIONS

(i) Assume that Dutch potatoes cost as much as British potatoes did 'a month ago'. How much could 'enterprising traders' gain by importing Dutch potatoes into Britain, at the time of the price differences?

(ii) Draw two supply and demand diagrams to show the changes in the markets for frozen chips in Britain, and Holland, in the period following the British government's action to raise prices.

(iii) Draw a production possibilities diagram, for production of potatoes or frozen chips, in Holland, to show the changes in production during the month in question.

(iv) Explain how the British government caused a black market in potatoes.

just over 500,000 tons through its agent, the Potato Marketing Board. But there was a snag here. This year, our market was supposed to be open to potatoes from other EEC countries. And what with the complexities of the Green Pound, Dutch farmers could undercut our guaranteed price, leaving us with a costly potato mountain. So the government banned imports from Holland.

Unfortunately, the Board had miscalculated. Housewives bought more potatoes than expected, and the market price shot up. According to the Board, the market price is now a reasonable £61 a ton and the British spud is in plentiful supply. But merchants and processors claim that they are desperately short and paid as much as £80 a ton last week, up to £27 on the price less than a month ago.

Meanwhile, the import ban has made the Dutch farmers furious and they have taken us to court. But the ban did not in any case cover processed potatoes, in other words frozen chips. So importers have been undercutting our chip processors, who have had to buy at higher market prices.

Unfortunately, many processors . . are now desperate. Most have had to stop production. One East Anglian firm has already laid off 60 staff, another 30. Both say more lay-offs are certain unless the government helps them.

Meanwhile, in another part of the Common Market, enterprising traders are successfully circumventing the import ban and making a lot of money out of the new artificial price difference. One merchant estimates that more than 300,000 tons of Dutch potatoes have been smuggled into Britain.

Clearly, a case of pommes de terres, laissez faire.

4 Trade — for or against

4.1 Gains from trade

'Possible gains from comparative advantage'

The gains that are possible from trade are no different in principle from the gains that follow from any specialisation. International specialisation that is based on differences in the comparative costs of production between countries will allow their resources to be used in the best of all possible ways.

In 1817, the economist David Ricardo explained this idea in the following way. He assumed that the number of man-years required by England and Portugal to produce cloth and wine respectively are:

	cloth	wine	
England	100	120	(number of man-years to
Portugal	90	80	produce one unit of each good)

Possible gains from comparative advantage

England may be so circumstanced that to produce the cloth may require the labour of 100 men for one year; and if she attempted to make the wine, it might require the labour of 120 men for the same time. England would therefore find it her interest to import wine, and to purchase it by the exportation of cloth.

To produce the wine in Portugal might require only the labour of 80 men for one year, and to produce the cloth in the same country might require the labour of 90 men for the same time. It would therefore be advantageous for her to export wine in exchange for cloth. This exchange might even take place notwithstanding that the commodity imported by Portugal could be produced there with less labour than in England. Though she could make the cloth with the labour of 90 men, she would import it from a country where it required the labour of 100 men to produce it, because it would be advantageous to her rather to employ her capital in the production of wine, for which she would obtain more cloth from England, than she could produce by diverting a portion of her capital from the cultivation of vines to the manufacture of cloth.

The opportunity cost of producing one unit of wine is, therefore, $\frac{12}{10}$ units of cloth in England, and $\frac{8}{9}$ of a unit of cloth in Portugal. Portugal can produce both goods more efficiently than England, but has a comparative advantage in the production of wine. This advantage allows gains to be made through specialisation and trade.

If each country specialises according to its comparative advantage, Portugal will produce wine and England will produce cloth. Before, it would have taken a total of 390 man-years for each country to produce one unit of each good. With specialisation, Portugal can produce two units of wine using 160 man-years, and England can produce two units of cloth using 200 man-years. The same four units of output can now be achieved from a total of 360 man-years. 30 man-years can be 'gained' by specialisation — 10 in Portugal, and 20 in England — and can be used to produce extra goods. Portugal can produce an extra $\frac{1}{8}$ of a unit of wine, and England an extra $\frac{1}{5}$ of a unit of cloth.

The size and distribution of gains

The size of the gains from trade will depend upon two things. On the one hand potential gains will be greater, the larger the difference between the comparative costs of countries. Two countries that possess very different factors of production, or produce under very different conditions, will therefore expect to gain the most from trade. On the other hand, there may be limitations which prevent countries from achieving all of their potential gains. Trading costs, or government restrictions, or costs in changing production, will all tend to reduce the amount of possible gain.

Any gains that are achieved will be distributed between countries. Between England and Portugal, for instance, the extra wine and cloth produced could eventually be consumed in either country, depending on the *terms of trade* which are set. Trade is unlikely to occur if it results in one country becoming worse off, but it might continue up to the point where all of the gains go to only one country.

If, before trade, each country had produced and consumed one unit of each good, then, after specialisation, at least the same amount would need to be made available through trade. The *extra* production ($\frac{1}{8}$ of a unit of wine, and $\frac{1}{5}$ of a unit of cloth) could, however, go various ways. For instance, if Portugal were to capture all of the gains from trade, and

England to remain no better off, then Portugal would need to exchange 1 unit of its production of wine, for $1\frac{1}{5}$ units of England's cloth.

Gains will also be distributed within each country. Some producers will gain more business and others less, and some factors of production will earn more income while others earn less. In the case of Portugal and England, it may well be that Portuguese wine-producers and English cloth-producers gain especially.

Free trade

Thomas Tooke: The 1820 Petition of the London Merchants

To the Honourable the Commons of Great Britain and Ireland:—
The Petition of, etc.
Humbly showeth,

That foreign commerce is eminently conducive to the wealth and prosperity of a country, by enabling it to import the commodities for the production of which the soil, climate, capital, and industry of other countries are best calculated, and to export in payment those articles for which its own situation is better adapted.

That freedom from restraint is calculated to give the utmost extension to foreign trade, and the best direction to the capital and industry of the country.

That the maxim of buying in the cheapest market, and selling in the dearest, which regulates every merchant in his individual dealings, is strictly applicable as the best rule for the trade of the whole nation.

That a policy founded on these principles would render the commerce of the world an interchange of mutual advantages, and diffuse an increase of wealth and enjoyments among the inhabitants of each State.

That, unfortunately, a policy the very reverse of this has been, and is, more or less, adopted and acted upon by the Government of this and of every other country, each trying to exclude the productions of other countries, with the specious and well-meant design of encouraging its own productions, thus inflicting on the bulk of its subjects who are consumers, the necessity of submitting to privations in the quantity or quality of commodities, and thus rendering what ought to be the source of mutual benefit and of harmony among States, a constantly-recurring occasion of jealousy and hostility.

(i) It is possible for all countries to gain by specialisation and trade according to their comparative advantage in production. The Merchants believed exactly this: that specialisation in 'articles for which its own situation is better adapted . . . is eminently conducive to the wealth and prosperity of a country'.

(ii) The extent to which gains are achieved will be limited by restrictions, such as government taxation, which inflict on 'consumers, . . . privations in the quantity or quality of commodities'.

(iii) Gains will be distributed between trading countries so that all will be better off than before trade, but some may gain more than others. This can cause, 'among States, a constantly-recurring occasion of jealousy and hostility'.

(iv) Gains will also be distributed between groups within each country. Dare we suggest that amongst those who might gain most from increased trade, we might expect to find the London Merchants themselves?

QUESTIONS

(i) Using Ricardo's figures, how would cloth and wine need to be traded in order for Portugal and England to consume equal amounts of each good after specialisation and trade?

(ii) Refer to the figures for farms A and B on page 10, and assume that they begin by each growing 100 acres of each crop. What would be the increase in their total production of both crops if they specialised completely according to comparative advantage?

(iii) How would the two farms need to trade, if farm B were to have exactly the same amount of each crop, as when growing 100 acres of each?

(iv) Suggest two considerations which might deter farms from specialising completely, despite the gains that are available.

'Free trade'

The 1820 Petition of the London Merchants was part of a campaign to persuade the British government to adopt a policy of 'free trade'. The arguments for and against this policy reflect each of the main issues arising from the gains from trade:

4.2 Losses from trade

Trade according to comparative advantage makes it possible for countries to gain the benefits of specialisation. Trade may also lead to losses, however, and these can be considered in four different areas.

The first difficulty is that there may be imperfections in the trading process, which, under free market forces, might lead to an inefficient use of resources. A second problem is that the line of specialisation that is required of a country may not be attractive to its citizens. Thirdly, it may be that trade leads to a distribution of income inside a country that is not acceptable to its citizens. Finally, trade might lead to a distribution of income between countries that is not acceptable to one of the partners.

'The best of British'

The sale of 'exclusive' goods and services to consumers from other countries is an example of international trade, based upon specialisation in production. Where the trade is in purely British products, such as public schools, or country houses, it will be due to an absolute advantage in production. Where it is in more humble products, such as jewellery, clothes or medical care, the trade is more likely to be explained by a comparative advantage in production.

Whatever its cause, and despite the increased income that it brings to Britain, this trade is not without its faults. It involves losses, as well as gains, for the people of Britain.

Imperfections

Some of the trade may be taking place in an inefficient way, without the justification of comparative cost differences. Since trade is caused by relative price differences, and since market imperfections might prevent prices reflecting real, opportunity costs, the trading process may be led astray. The main imperfections to intrude in this way will include 'unrealistic' exchange rates for countries' currencies, dominant buyers or sellers in a market, and government taxes or subsidies.

A Russian Beriozka store is trading under as strong an imperfection as one can imagine. Only foreign consumers are allowed to shop there, at prices set artificially low by the authorities. A less extreme, but similar example is found in the market for medical care in Britain if, as seems probable, some part of the training of medical staff has been subsidised by the government. In each case prices will tend to be lower than if set by comparative costs

The best of British (but it's not for us)

Last time I was in Moscow I wanted to buy something particularly Russian for friends back home.

Simple! I just went along to what's called a Beriozka store. It was full of typically Russian products like beluga caviare, canned sturgeon, smoked salmon, the finest vodka, sumptuous furs.

Not so typically Russian were my fellow shoppers: Japanese businessmen, American tourists, British diplomats' wives.

The typical Russian himself, the ordinary citizen, was just as typically absent: the best examples of his country's products were exclusively reserved for 'hard currency' foreigners like me.

Indeed, he'd find that his way into the shop was barred by another typically Russian institution, a doorman the size of a padded meat safe.

Even if he'd been allowed through the door, the average Ivan's salary would not have been enough to pay for the goodies inside.

. . . Unlike the Russians and the Chinese, we're not officially barred from buying the best of what's typically British.

Or are we? Could it be that as in the Marxist States whole areas of our national life are, in effect, being turned into such Beriozka stores, where only foreign money is welcome because only foreign wallets can disgorge sufficient pelf?

Jewellery shops, furniture stores and fashion houses are all growing fat on foreign money.

Harrods — once the local store for the British middle classes — now advertises its sale in Arabic papers and has become virtually an overseas souk for the United Arab Emirates. . . .

In none of these emporia can there be any incentive for prices to be kept down to fit British purses when the pickings from foreigners can be so high.

A current top-selling line in the new British Beriozka is the public school. Despite all political pressures, this unique institution is flourishing.

British middle-class noses are still pressed up

alone, and the specialisation and trade that follow will result in a misuse of resources.

Specialisation

There are several reasons why the citizens of a country may object to the pattern of specialisation required by the principle of comparative advantage. They may object to the production of certain goods such as arms or nuclear development on ethical or political grounds. They may object to close economic

against the glass, hoping desperately to scrape together enough cash to enable their little Nigels and Jeremys to benefit from a sturdy dose of good schooling and sound discipline.

But increasingly it's not the little Jeremys and Nigels trooping through the hallowed doors with their set-squares and rugger boots. They're being elbowed aside by little Khaleds and Mohammeds, whose oil-rich parents are touchingly anxious to shell out the ryals for British cricket, cold baths and 1066-and-all-that.

Boarding fees at Britain's top public schools now average £2,000 a year, and this month a new agency has been set up to deal with the vast increase in applications for places from foreign pupils. . . .

And what else is there gleaming on the shelves of the British Beriozka? Well, Britain has an international reputation for the integrity and high standards of its medical care. . . .

But Britain also has hospital waiting-lists. So despite all political pressures, private medicine is flourishing. The British increasingly want to buy — hence the growth in health insurance schemes.

But thanks to the phasing out of pay beds in National Health hospitals, there's a new boom in the building of private hospitals — in 1976 40 new ones were built in England alone, and fees in these establishments can reach over £100 a day. . . .

Needless to say, it's the Arabs who can afford to spend most freely on this particular British goodie — it's estimated that the Kuwaitis and Libyans alone spend over £6½ million a year on getting medical treatment here. It is too costly for the British.

Our national shelves are loaded more and more with goods labelled 'for foreign buyers only.' Art treasures, country mansions, town houses.

Once upon a time, a moderately well-off couple could afford to rent a decent flat in a 'good' area of London. Now, thanks to the Rent Act — and money from foreign tourists looking for a holiday base in London — even a relatively modest three-bedroom flat in Maida Vale can be let to overseas visitors for £500 a week.

Like I said, we're turning ourselves into a Beriozka store for international shoppers.

inter-dependence with other countries, or to the risk of a loss of future income, if they depend too much upon the export of one product. They may object to the process of change required in taking up a new pattern of specialisation, if this involves unemployment, relocation, and disruption of the economic system. For all of these reasons, the British may object to specialising more and more in the production of jewellery shops, public schools and fashion houses.

Income distribution

The changing pattern of specialisation and trade will affect the distribution of income within the country. As a whole, the British may object if those selling prestige goods in London benefit much more than others. Similarly they may object if foreigners seem to be gaining relatively more from the process of trade: if the British buy oil, but the Arabs buy 'the best of British' goods and services.

In either case it would be an irrational act to forgo all the benefits from trade, in order to avoid these losses — an act of 'cutting off the nose to spite the face'! Rather, it should be possible to adjust the distribution of gains, and satisfy all parties.

Policy

All objections to trade fall under one of two headings. Either they are objections because the trading system is not working as well as it could, in which case the implication for policy is clearly to try to introduce some improvement. Alternatively, they are objections because the system is working well, but is producing an unacceptable result. Here, the implication for policy is to restrict trade or to balance any undesirable results.

QUESTIONS

(i)   Which of the losses from trade described in the text follow because (a) the trade system is working only imperfectly, (b) the trade system is leading to an undesirable result?

(ii)   What differences are there between the ways consumers are discouraged from buying their typical, national products in Britain and Russia?

(iii)   Of the typically Russian, and typically British products described in the extract, which are
(a) primary products (agriculture, fishing, mining etc);
(b) secondary products (manufactured goods);
(c) tertiary products (services)?

(iv)   How can the different pattern of specialisation described in your answer to the last question be explained by the different types of factors found in each country?

(v)   Suggest two losses, from Britain's point of view, that might follow from the trade between Britain and Portugal described on page 16.

4.3 Protection

'Time for the chop'

Government policy on trade will either try to make the process work better, or will try to limit undesirable effects upon production and consumption. Protection of a domestic industry against foreign competition can be for either of these reasons. Of which kind are the arguments for protecting British Leyland car production from Japanese competition?

Time for the chop

Japanese car makers are poised to give British Leyland a karate chop.

Last month their imports were 130 per cent up on a year ago. British Leyland's market share sagged again.

Japan ignored its undertaking to restrict sales – and talks on pegging its imports this year have broken down.

The Japanese car industry was ruthlessly shielded from competition until it was ready to take on the world.

Without similar protection British Leyland could be a dead duck before its planned new models reach the showrooms.

Italy limited Japanese sales to 2,000 cars in 1976. Britain needn't go that far.

But if taxpayers are to see any return on the £246 million already pumped into Leyland there must be restrictions.

Some Japanese sales would no doubt go to Renault, Fiat and Volkswagen. But Common Market prosperity is more likely to rub off on Britain.

The best way to avoid a karate chop is to take a few lessons in self defence.

Protection to balance imperfections

The free trade system can work perfectly only if prices reflect real, relative scarcity. If an imperfection of any kind distorts price levels, then it will not be possible for international trade to take full benefit from the principle of comparative advantage. Is it possible that the prices of Japanese cars are lower than they should be, on the basis of comparative costs of production alone? There are two reasons for thinking that this might be so.

We are told that 'the Japanese car industry was ruthlessly shielded from competition' in the past. If the policy of the Japanese government is still to assist their car industry, or if Japanese car firms can subsidise their export sales by keeping prices high in a protected home market, then British firms will have

a case for claiming that they are facing unfair competition.

In addition, it would be possible for the prices of all Japanese products to be lower than expected, on the basis of comparative costs. This would result if the exchange rate of Japanese currency for other currencies was set, through government intervention, at a level lower than that chosen by long-term market forces. All Japanese exports would then appear to be relatively cheap on world markets, even if they cost as much to make in terms of real resources.

Protection of an infant industry

An infant industry is one that has yet to grow up. British Leyland is of an age that this would need to be at least its second childhood! Nevertheless, it may well lack development, as an international car firm, in certain ways.

An industry will deserve protecting in its early years, if it will be able to produce at a comparative advantage once it has developed. Its costs may be comparatively high at the start, but they must be able to become lower than in competing countries, when it is fully mature. Such development will only be possible if there are economies of scale, which will reduce the relative unit costs of the firm, as it grows. There are significant economies of scale in the production of cars, and it was for this reason that the Japanese car industry was protected 'until it was ready to take on the world'.

The same argument could well be applied to British Leyland, but there would be difficulties. One problem is that comparative costs of production might not improve as much as expected. Economies of scale would change the pattern of comparative advantage, but in a way that could not be known in advance. Another problem is that once under government protection, the industry might lose the incentive to develop in the way that was intended. As a result it might never be clear when protection should be removed — whether the infant has completely grown up!

Protection to prevent unemployment

A change in the pattern of comparative advantage will encourage a move along each country's production possibilities frontier. Resources will be transferred out of the production of one good and into production of another. If British Leyland has lost its comparative advantage in the production of cars to the Japanese, its resources will be transferred into alternative work, and its output of cars will drop. This will involve a move from one production possibility to another, as shown in diagram 1, from point A to point C. So why should there be any unemployment?

Unfortunately, resources are not often employed as quickly as they are laid off. Both the capital and the labour that has been employed by British Leyland has become skilled in particular types of work, and concentrated in certain areas. It is not often possible to provide similar work in the same area, in new expanding industries.

The process of specialisation according to a change

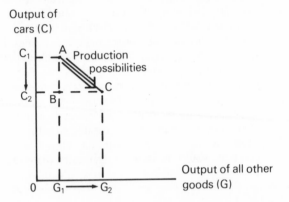

Diagram 1   The effect of a change in comparative advantage upon car production

in comparative advantage can, therefore, be an unpleasant one for the country concerned. The decline in one industry, such as cars, will often be seen for some time before there is an equal expansion in another. In the meanwhile there will be unemployment, as shown by the movement inside the frontier of production possibilities, in diagram 1, from point A to point B.

Protection can delay, smooth out, or prevent this process. Such a policy will also imply a loss of the possible gains from trade but, in order to help the particular industry concerned, and to keep the country's distribution of income in their favour, such a choice may well be made.

Protection of a strategic industry

Specialisation according to comparative advantage may require a country to end production of various 'strategic' goods. To protect its political independence a country may refuse to do this. Industries such as agriculture, steel, and armaments are often protected for this reason, and car production might also be included. Certainly it is the case that British Leyland plays a strategic role in the economic structure of the country, in that so many other types of production and employment are indirectly linked to it.

Protection to influence each country's gains from trade

In special circumstances, a country may be fortunate enough to be able to turn the terms of trade in its favour. By so doing it will be able to redistribute the overall gains from world trade, away from other countries, and to its own advantage.

This is not a power that could be used by British Leyland, but there is, nevertheless, one way in which the distribution of income between countries would be affected by their protection. Protection against Japanese imports would allow European car firms to gain in the British market, and since 'Common Market prosperity is more likely to rub off on Britain', more of the gains from trade would come Britain's way.

How to protect?

British Leyland could be protected from Japanese competition in several ways. A tariff on Japanese cars would raise their price on the British market, so discouraging consumers from buying them. An import quota would restrict the quantity of cars imported each year and could be imposed by the manufacturers themselves, or by government order. A subsidy on British Leyland cars would reduce their price on the home market and give them a competitive advantage over all imported cars.

QUESTIONS

(i)   Which of the five arguments listed in the text for protecting British Leyland are intended to (a) make the trading system work better, (b) prevent the outcome of a perfect trading system?

(ii)   Which of the five arguments for protecting British Leyland imply that protection should be (a) temporary, (b) permanent?

(iii)   Assume that two countries produce two goods under economies of scale, but have identical production possibilities. When each country produces each good equally is there any comparative advantage? Are there any benefits possible from specialisation, and if so, for which country in which good?

(iv)   Which forms of protection for cars are described in the extract for (a) Italy, (b) British Leyland?

(v)   In what sense will British Leyland become a 'dead duck' if it is not protected?

5 International payments

5.1 Types of international payments

'Exporting rail'

Britain was one of the first countries to develop a railway industry, and so gained an absolute advantage in production. Even when other countries developed their own industries it was possible for Britain to keep a comparative advantage, and to continue a high level of trade with the rest of the world. This trade was of various kinds, and caused a variety of types of payments both in and out of Britain.

Payments for goods

Goods that are produced at home, and then sold to consumers in other countries, are described as *visible exports*. When these goods leave their country of origin a corresponding payment will be paid in to the country. Exports of goods will, therefore, bring a gain in terms of payments. This two-way exchange is illustrated in diagram 1.

Visible exports by the British railway industry in the nineteenth century took the form of hardware and equipment. Robert Stephenson & Co produced locomotives in Britain, and exported them 'to Austria, Belgium, France...' and most other countries! Rails were manufactured in Britain, and exported 'in sizeable quantities... for lines being thrust across America'. All of these visible exports of products brought a flow of payments into Britain and into the pockets of the manufacturers concerned.

Although these types of exports were all the result of production by British industry, they would, in the main, become part of the capital structure of the countries buying them. With its railway system, a country would be able to transport materials and

---

Exporting rail

The existence of a practicable railway technology in Britain in the early 1830s, in advance of other countries, quickly resulted in the purchase of British equipment by European and United States railways. By 1840 the locomotive builders, Robert Stephenson & Co, had supplied engines to Austria, Belgium, France, Germany, Italy, Russia and North America....

But more than hardware was being exported. The great, and undervalued, civil engineer Joseph Locke was responsible for the construction of continental railways early in the Railway Age. Locke was the engineer for the Paris-Rouen line (1841-43), the railway between Rouen and Le Havre (1843) and parts of the Spanish and Dutch systems.

Allied to this management skill, British railway contractors were also pushing railways through a number of countries. In the 1840s Thomas Brassey, for instance, had contracts in six European countries and India, Canada, Australia, Mauritius, Argentina, Russia and Romania....

The fast growth of railways the world over led to the establishment of indigenous railway manufacturing industry. Even so, such was the demand for railway equipment that Britain was able to export sizable quantities of rails for lines being thrust across America. In 1867, 15,000 tons of rails were exported from Britain to the United States. By 1871, 500,000 tons were moving westwards over the ocean and, in

the early 1880s, the Americans were purchasing more than a million tons in a year from Britain.

By the 1870s most of the British network was complete and a different pattern now developed. Conveniently, railway development in India had really only built up steam by the late 1870s. The lessening opportunities for investment in British industry at the beginning of this period saw a significant switch, with capital being deployed to overseas railway development, most significantly in Argentina where railway activities also took in ports construction, power stations and river steamers. All told, Argentine railways constituted the largest British commercial enterprise outside the United Kingdom and the British Empire.

The beauty of railway construction lay in the derived demand for locomotives, rolling stock, track, signalling and workshop equipment. For every new locomotive there were the corresponding machine tools needed in the workshop maintaining it. In today's terms the sums involved in construction were vast – up to 1872-73 nearly 6,000 miles of railway were laid down in India at a cost of almost £100m.

The sheer scale of demand for railway equipment saw the establishment of an extensive, complicated and well-versed management capability consisting of British consulting engineers, agents, and British-trained engineering and operating managers – all required to construct and maintain the railways of the Empire.

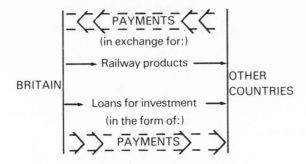

Diagram 1   International payments for rail

people, and increase its own production of other goods. Developing countries would, therefore, be eager to convert their liquid capital, held in the form of money, into physical capital in the form of imported railway equipment. Where they had raised their money from in the first place, is a question that we shall consider shortly.

Payments for services

Services that are produced at home, and then sold to consumers in other countries are described as *invisible exports*. Although there may be no tangible end-product, services are the result of a production process, and give satisfaction to the consumer, quite as much as visible goods. They will again earn payments for their producers.

Britain exported a good deal of technical and managerial skill in the nineteenth century. Other countries paid for the services of construction engineers, contractors, agents, and operating managers, who gave advice, and administered work, on the construction of railways throughout the world. Joseph Locke, for example, was responsible for the lines built between Paris and Rouen and Rouen and Le Havre, and Thomas Brassey had contracts in 'six European countries'.

The earnings brought back to Britain by all of these individuals would have become payments in to the country for invisible exports.

Payments of money capital

Payments from one country to another, that are not in exchange for any visible or invisible products, are known as transfers of money capital. These payments are different in nature from the payments made for products. In the trade of a product, payment is made in exchange for goods and services. In a payment of money capital, by contrast, payment is made as a loan of purchasing potential. This means that when loans leave a country, there is a payment out of the

country, but when products leave a country, there is a payment in.

Another difference is that funds are usually transferred only temporarily, and will be returned to their owners at a later date. If so, the payment of money capital out of a country will later be followed by an inward flow of payments, as returns are earned on it, and as the original sum is repaid. It is important to notice that these returns are payments for the work done by the factor while out of the country, and therefore paid for the service it has provided. The original outflow will have been a payment of money capital, but the inflow of returns will be for 'invisible' production.

British capital was invested in the railway development of other countries on a grand scale, in the years after 1870. 'Argentine railways constituted the largest British commercial enterprise outside the United Kingdom and the British Empire' and vast sums were invested in India. All of this investment required payments out of Britain, but the years ever since then have seen payments back into Britain in the form of interest, profits and dividends, as invisible earnings on that investment.

Here, perhaps, we find one source of the money which other countries used to buy British equipment and expertise, in the years of railway development. To some extent, funds were transferred out of Britain in the form of loans, to be returned back into Britain as payments for the exports of visible and invisible railway production. This partly explains the circular flow of payments that is illustrated in diagram 1.

QUESTIONS

In each of the following cases, say whether there will have been a direct payment in or out of Britain, and whether it will be for (a) visible trade, (b) invisible trade, or (c) as a flow of money capital:

(i)   a British steamer is sold to Argentina;
(ii)   a British government loan is made to the Argentinian government;
(iii)   British machine tools are sold to Canadian railways;
(iv)   British train drivers are employed by Canadian railways;
(v)   British signalling equipment is sold to Indian railways;
(vi)   a British design for a signalling system is sold to Indian railways;
(vii)   credit is granted by British firms to customers in France.

5.2 The effects of international payments

Payments are made between countries either in exchange for traded products, or as loans. A loan of money capital will allow a country to increase its spending on goods and services from abroad, and so, in turn, give rise to corresponding but opposite payments in trade. This flow of payments between countries was illustrated in the last section. Capital investment by Britain in the railways of other countries was used to pay for British exports of railway products. It is those payments made directly for traded products, therefore, that we must study in order to see the effects such payments have upon both the economy of the country which pays and the economy of the country which receives payment.

Output and employment

An inward payment is an injection of demand into a country's economy and adds to its circular flow of income. An outward payment is a leakage and subtracts from it. National output is, in equilibrium, the same as national income and will tend to rise as a result of inward payments, but to fall as a result of outward payments.

Employment is set, in the main, by the level of output in the economy. It will rise when the general level of demand encourages output to rise, and will fall when demand becomes depressed.

The flow of payments made in exchange for traded goods and services in and out of the country will strike a balance that can be in either surplus or deficit. When that balance of payments is in surplus it will cause the levels of output and employment in the economy to rise. When it is in deficit, it will lead them to fall.

The strength of this influence will depend upon the size of the surplus or deficit; on its multiplied effect upon sectors of the economy not directly involved in trade; and on any changes in other sources of demand in the economy that happen at the same time.

The nature of its impact can also differ from case to case, depending upon the types of trade payments made. Payments for consumption goods will generate one pattern of demand, and payments for capital goods another. Capital investment will allow an economy to produce more output in the future, but only at the expense of a lower level of consumption for the present.

Many of these effects are illustrated for the New Zealand economy, in an adverse way, in the example that follows.

Bad for New Zealand; costly for us

New Zealand is increasingly worried about the future of the all-important trade in mutton and lamb with Britain. Since last December New Zealand cheese has ceased to be sold in the EEC. The prospect for butter is the same. The Irish are urging in Brussels that New Zealand has no longer any right to its quarter of the British market and plans to replace New Zealand's leading Anchor brand with Irish Kerrigold at higher prices. Under the transitional arrangements New Zealand was resigned to a token share in dairy products sales. But it believed on the sheer facts of the supply position it would be left with its export of over 200,000 tons of "sheepmeat"....

It is not just the sale of the 200,000 tons that are at stake (or the little matter of Britain's £500m investment in the trade, the butchers' interests not included). The entire New Zealand sheep industry, including its wool trade, would be faced with drastic scaling down – and it provides a third of the national income. There is no alternative market yet. The potential of the country – its potential to provide cheap protein in a needy if autarkic world, would be stultified. Already unemployment soars and New Zealanders emigrate. The political implications are considerable.

New Zealand

Britain and New Zealand have long enjoyed a close relationship which, despite the 12 000 miles that separate them, has been reflected in their high level of trade. In line with the principle of comparative advantage this trade has allowed New Zealand to import a wide range of manufactured goods in exchange for its exports of agricultural products. By the end of the 1960s, Britain was taking a quarter of all New Zealand's exports, and 90% of her butter, 75% of her cheese, and 86% of her lamb. But in 1973, Britain joined the European Economic Community.

A central feature of EEC policy, and one that Britain had to accept in order to become a full member of the Community, is the aim of self-sufficiency in food production. After a period of transition, imports of food from outside the EEC would be expected to end. New Zealand would no longer be able to trade the same goods to the same extent to the British market. Whatever the arguments for or against this agricultural policy might be from Britain's point of view, it could have only a disastrous effect upon the New Zealand economy.

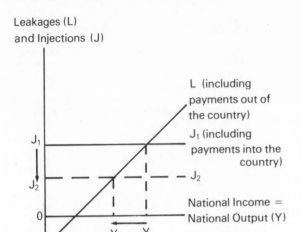

Leakages (L)
and Injections (J)

L (including payments out of the country)

J_1 (including payments into the country)

J_2

National Income = National Output (Y)

Y_2 Y_1

If payments into the country decrease, other things remaining equal, national output and employment tend to fall.

Diagram 1   The effect of international payments upon national output

Unemployment soars

By the end of the 1970s, New Zealand had already lost much of its market for cheese and butter, and faced a similar threat to its export of 'sheepmeat'. Payments into the country from its sale of agricultural exports had fallen greatly, and had affected output, income, and employment within the economy.

A fall in export earnings, other things being equal, represents a fall in the demand for goods and services within an economy, and in the level of injections into the circular flow of income. The level of economic activity drops, and with it, the demand for labour. The economy suffers from unemployment and a slump in output, of the kind shown in diagram 1.

New Zealand is especially dependent upon the sheep industry for its livelihood. The fall in payments to this sector, which 'provides a third of the national income' would cause a depression on a great scale. Its multiplied effect would be felt in all types of industry, and all lines of work within New Zealand.

Is there any way in which these results might be avoided? New Zealand's hopes rest with the other types of injections and leakages in the circular flow of income. Injections might be raised sufficiently to offset the loss of export payments, through the growth of alternative markets, or the expansion of government support. Leakages would be cut if domestic consumers chose to spend less of their income on imported goods.

These hopes are not unrealistic, but they are unlikely to match the scale of the problem facing New Zealand. Even if alternative sources of demand could be found in order to maintain the levels of output and employment in New Zealand, this would still bring long-term changes in the economy. The structure of demand would fall on different types of goods, and bring prosperity to different sectors. Any fall in imports would restrict New Zealand's access to the variety of goods, services, and capital equipment offered in the rest of the world. It is no wonder that the restriction of trading opportunities to Britain should be described as bad for New Zealand.

QUESTIONS

(i)   Suppose that the EEC introduces regulations to ban all imports of New Zealand butter. Predict the effects of this change upon the *Irish* economy.

(ii)   Explain briefly the ways in which the loss of New Zealand imports of food is costly for Britain.

(iii)   Suggest three policies, other than an import ban, which the EEC might introduce in order to replace New Zealand with Irish butter in the British market.

(iv)   How would the loss of markets for New Zealand's exports of food affect the price of wool in the world?

25

6 The balance of payments

6.1 The official reserves

Every country will hold reserves of international currencies other than its own. For most countries these reserves will include gold, and United States dollars, as well as any other currencies that are likely to be used by the country for international payments.

As with any holding of money, there is an opportunity cost directly associated with the official reserves. Money can be exchanged for goods and services, and international money can be exchanged for the output of other countries. A country could be better off in terms of real goods and services if it spent its official reserves, and is deliberately giving up those benefits by holding on to them. What are its reasons for doing so?

Why hold reserves?

Official reserves are kept for a 'transactions motive', because the money may be needed for spending at some stage in the future. This will be when the authorities buy and sell in order to influence exchange rates in the markets for international currencies. Their reasons for intervening are considered in chapter 9; for the present it will be sufficient to ask only how their action affects the reserves.

At a given exchange rate, all payments in and out of the country will be matched, on balance, by changes in the reserves. If more is being paid out than in, the reserves will fall. If more is being paid in than out, the reserves will rise.

If the reserves were not available as 'stocks' in this way, then intended levels of payment would set the exchange rate, from moment to moment. The authorities might choose to use the reserves to smooth out short-term fluctuations, or to set the exchange rate at a level of their own invention. In either case, as the reserves change, they provide a direct measure of the overall balance of payments they are being used to offset.

'Nice timing by Treasury'

We will consider here the behaviour of the United

Nice timing by Treasury

The timing of the repayment to the International Monetary Fund last month could scarcely have been better. The transfer was made in a package of currencies, including actual dollars and a chunk of special drawing rights from the United Kingdom reserves. These drawing rights were on the books at $1.20635 but were sold back to the IMF at the then market rate of $1.326.

This gave the reserves a nominal saving of about $20 million and makes it possible to deduce that special drawing rights involved amounted to about 150 million.

The total cost of the repayment took only $980 million out of the total United Kingdom reserves last month, expressed in dollar terms. Against this payment, the reserves received $350 million from the Electricity Council loan as expected, plus $18 million borrowed by the National Coal Board from the European Coal and Steel Community.

Repayments under Treasury guarantees totalled $35 million made up of a number of small public sector loan payments. The reserves should therefore have fallen by $647 million on the basis of these visible transactions. In fact the published loss during October is $540 million which implies a net inflow during the month of $107 million covering invisible and visible trade payments, capital accounts, run-of-the-mill Government capital payments and vital flows of hot money across the exchanges financed by the Bank of England.

The figures imply that on balance the Bank of England left the exchange rate very largely to find its own level last month, intervening to buy dollars and hold sterling down on a very small scale, certainly in comparison with the $2,500 million which Dr Emminger said yesterday the Bundesbank had bought last month.

The authorities are more than usually tight lipped at the moment, but certainly did nothing yesterday to upset the conclusion that the Bank has not intervened on a big scale.

Kingdom reserves one October. It was at this time that the Treasury needed to make a payment of $980 million out of the country, to return a loan of capital to the International Monetary Fund. It was important for them to choose a month in which other payments would, on balance, bring a substantial amount into the country. Only if this were so could the reserves afford such a large outward payment, without undue strain. Why did the Treasury show such 'nice timing' in choosing October?

Trade payments

Many other international payments were also being made at that time. Trade in 'visible' goods and 'invisible' services will have caused a great deal of payment in each direction. Loans by private individuals and companies, for short-term speculation and long-term investment, will also have passed each way. 'Run of the mill Government capital payments' will have been a third source of payments in and out of the country. The reserves cannot register each of these payments individually, but only the overall net balance that results from them. It appears that, in October, this balance was for $107 million more to be paid into the country, than was paid out. The reserves rose accordingly.

A further benefit to the reserves at this time came from government payments that were far from being run of the mill. Although the Treasury had to make an outward payment of $35 million, this was more than offset by inward flows of $368 borrowed by the Electricity Council and the National Coal Board.

On balance

The impact of all the different types of payments upon the official reserves is summarised in the table. It shows that, on balance, the reserves would have increased by $440 million in the month of October, if the Treasury had not chosen to make its official repayment to the IMF. The relative strength of the reserves allowed them to do so without too much strain, and explained the 'nice timing' of their decision.

The actual fall in the reserves of $540 million followed because the authorities were buying sterling to offset the effect of a payments deficit. This will have kept the exchange rate higher than it would otherwise have been.

Nevertheless, the scale of this spending is slight, by comparison with past experience. This suggests that, 'on balance, the Bank of England left the exchange rate very largely to find its own level'.

QUESTIONS

(i) What two types of international currency are mentioned in the extract?

(ii) What would have been the change in the reserves in October if the UK had been allowed to repay half of its loan to the IMF in terms of pound sterling, instead of dollars?

(iii) What would have been the effect, from the intervention by the German Bundesbank in the currency markets in October, on (a) Germany's official reserves, (b) the exchange rate of the Deutschemark for the US dollar?

(iv) What will have been the main effects of the Electricity Council's loan on the UK reserves in October *and* in the years following?

Table 1   Changes in the UK Reserves in October

Net inflow from:	+ (addition to reserves)	− (subtraction from reserves)

Visible and Invisible Trade
Private Capital flows
  (short-term and long-term)
Government Capital flows
  ("run-of-the-mill")
	107	

Government Capital flows (special payments)	350 18	35
Balance = 440		
Official Repayments to the International Monetary Fund		980
Overall change in Reserves: Balance =		540

All figures in $ million

27

6.2 The structure of the accounts

A country will keep an account of the flow of international payments that pass across its borders, over a given period of time. These *balance of payments accounts* are structured in two ways.

First, they will pay respect to the different types of payments that are made, by measuring each in a different section of the accounts. Secondly, they will show the final balance of all payments, as a surplus or deficit, in two different ways. One will be to add up all the individual payments, and the other will be to take the change in the level of official reserves, or their equivalent.

The balance of payments in 1974 and 1975

Current account payments are all made in exchange for products that are traded in and out of the country. A distinction is drawn between those payments that are made for the visible trade in goods, and others that are made for the invisible trade in services.

In both 1974 and 1975 there was a net surplus on invisible trade that was more than outweighed by a net deficit on visible trade. The current account was, therefore, in deficit both years.

Investment and other capital flows include all loans, whether for short-term speculation or long-term investment, and whether by private bodies or by government. On balance, these payments were in surplus in 1974, but they moved into deficit in 1975.

The overall balance of payments, found by combining these two sections of the accounts, was in deficit in each year. The direct effect of this deficit is

Table 1   Balance of payments (£ millions)

	1974	1975
Current account		
Visible trade balance	−5,264	−3,200
Invisible balance	+1,653	+1,500
Current balance	−3,611	1,700
Investment and other capital flows	+1,582	−708
Balancing item	+357	+929
Balance for official financing	−1,672	−1,479
Official financing		
Foreign currency borrowing by HM Government and the public sector	+1,751	+810
Official reserves (drawings on/additions to −)	−79	+669
Total official financing	+1,672	+1,479

[Source: *Bank of England Quarterly Bulletin* Vol 16 No 2, June 1976, Table 19]

seen in the *Official financing* section of the accounts, for this shows the changes in official reserves, or in special loan arrangements with international bodies. In both 1974 and 1975 there was heavy official borrowing from other countries, and in 1975 there was also a substantial reduction in the reserves.

QUESTIONS

(i)   The UK balance of payments deficit was about the same, overall, in 1974 and 1975. How did the reasons for this deficit change?

(ii)   Under which of the headings in the balance of payments accounts would each of the following payments (which each refer to previous extracts) appear?
(a) payments for UK exports of rails
(b) payments for UK engineers working abroad
(c) increased credit offered by UK companies to German companies
(d) official loan repayments to the IMF.

The oil crisis

The oil crisis of 1973 and 1974 arose when the Organisation of Petroleum Exporting Countries (OPEC) used their monopoly power at first to restrict supply, but then to raise the price of crude oil fourfold. This had a serious effect upon output, employment and prices throughout the oil-importing world, and was also blamed for causing a crisis in the United Kingdom's balance of payments.

The cost to the UK of importing crude oil jumped from £171 million in the first quarter of 1973 to £684 million in the first quarter of 1974. The statistics in table 2 show that the trade deficit due to imports of oil was £3.4 billion in 1974, and £3.1 billion in 1975. This burden was critical not only because of its size, but also because of the suddenness with which it struck.

But is this the whole story? It seems unlikely, since it takes into consideration only those payments made for the visible trade in oil. There are many other sections to the balance of payments accounts which may also have been affected.

Payments into the United Kingdom

Extra payments made to OPEC are part of an international flow of income. Some of this income might well have been returned to the UK, depending upon how OPEC chose to use it.

In 1974, the total amount paid to OPEC for their oil was about £40.1 billion (see table 2). Some of this income they saved, to give them a 'surplus' of £24.5

Table 2   Payments between the UK and OPEC in 1974 and 1975

		(£000 million)	
		1974	1975
	Visible Trade: oil imports into UK	−3.4	−3.1
(Estimated oil revenues of OPEC)		(40.1)	(46.2)
	Visible Trade: exports to OPEC from UK	+ 1.2	+ 2.3
(Estimated surpluses of OPEC)		(24.5)	(14.6)
(of which, amount deployed in UK)		(9.1)	(1.9)
	Amount of surpluses converted to sterling investments	+ 2.6	0.0
	BALANCE on visible trade and capital account	+ 0.4	−0.8

Notes: (1) Payments into the UK are +, payments to OPEC are −.
(2) Exchange rates taken as £1 : $2.34 in 1974, and £1 : $2.20 in 1975.

Sources: (i) *Bank of England Quarterly Bulletin* Vol 16, No 2, June 1976 Table 19.
(ii) *Bank of England Quarterly Bulletin* Vol 16, No 2, June 1976 p175
(iii) *Monthly Digest of Statistics* No 376 April 1977, CSO, Table 14.7
(iv) *Annual Abstract of Statistics*, CSO, 1976

ever, for in 1975 the net effect was reversed to a payments deficit of £0.8 billion.

QUESTIONS

(i)   Describe the main changes in the pattern of payments between the UK and OPEC, from 1974 to 1975.
(ii)   Briefly suggest a possible explanation for each of those changes.
(iii)   Explain whether the UK would prefer to receive an equivalent amount from OPEC on current account, or capital account.

billion. The rest they spent, to the sum of (£40.1 − £24.5 =) £15.6 billion. A reasonable amount of that spending − £1.2 billion in fact − was spent on visible goods exported by the UK.

In addition, a large part of their surplus was brought to the UK for safe-keeping, in bank accounts and loans. £2.6 billion of this they converted into sterling investments, and the rest they kept in terms of other currencies. Their sterling investments entered the UK balance of payments as capital inflows, and the work provided for the financial service industries of the UK earned 'invisible' payments.

Taking as many of these payments into account as possible, it appears that far from being in 'critical' deficit in 1974, the UK balance of payments gained a net surplus of at least £0.4 billion! By some irony, the oil crisis had actually helped the balance of payments of the UK. This situation was not to last, how-

7 Balance of payments policy

7.1 The need for policy

So many payments pass in and out of a country that they will not often strike a perfect balance, and the direct impact of this, at a given exchange rate, will fall on the level of official reserves.

Given the right conditions, a payments imbalance can be corrected by the forces of the free market. A payments deficit, for instance, will encourage a country's prices to fall relative to those elsewhere, by means of either a fall in the exchange rate, or deflation in the domestic economy. Even so the reserves will have to be able to absorb imbalances in the period until the process is completed: perhaps several years.

A persistent surplus on the balance of payments will cause the reserves to grow too large. This will bring too great an opportunity cost, in terms of the extra goods that could be bought. A continuing deficit will cause the reserves to become too small, or even run out, and so restrict the country's trade. Either situation will prompt the government to introduce a balance of payments policy.

'When the reserves run out!'

For year after year, Turkey had been suffering from a deficit on its payments for trade in goods and services. To some extent this 'overspending' could be financed by borrowing from other countries, to bring payments of money capital in to the country. Even so, the country's official reserves decreased steadily, from over $2000 million to only $600 million, over five years (see chart 1). In the end, Turkey 'ran out of hard currency and stopped paying for imports'. The country could not pay its international debts, and could no longer continue to trade freely.

A government will usually introduce policies, in advance, to prevent this situation occurring. The 'devaluation' and 'austerity programme' were policies introduced by the Turkish government to begin an improvement in the balance of payments 'this year'.

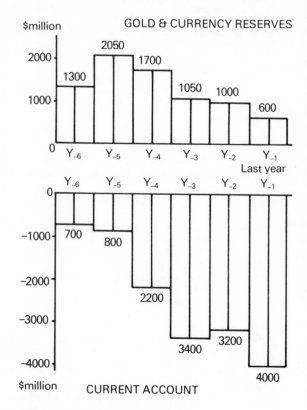

Chart 1   When the reserves run out!

When the reserves run out!

With today's devaluation Turkey has completed the basic elements of its austerity programme...

The announcement of the devaluation almost coincided with the first anniversary of the day Turkey ran out of hard currency and stopped paying for imports outside the strategic and emergency category. Unpaid imports last year probably exceeded $1.5bn. and the country has defaulted on more than $400m. worth of bankers' loans. Another $1bn. of such loans will mature this year. These figures alone demonstrate the depth of the crisis facing the Government. But there are many others: the current account deficit last year was a staggering $4bn.

QUESTIONS

(i)   Calculate, from the chart, in which of the 'last five years' Turkey borrowed more than it paid back to other countries.
(ii)   Assuming that the current account deficit remains the same as 'last year', what reserves would Turkey need to pay all its debts 'this year'?
(iii)   What would have been the effect of a persistent payments deficit on output and employment in Turkey over the 'last five years'?

7.2 The policy alternatives

If a country is suffering from a continuing imbalance in the payments for its trade in products, it can accommodate this situation in two ways. It can balance its current account payments with its net payments of money capital, or it can allow its reserves to bear the weight of adjustment. Both of these responses, however, are only temporary answers to the problem. They buy time until a more permanent solution is found, either through market forces or by government policy.

Balance of payments policy is intended to affect the size of payments made for products traded in and out of the country. This will involve changing the amount, or the prices, of those products. Each type of change will be effected by particular types of policies.

Each type of policy will affect other areas of the economy, besides the balance of international payments. In particular, there is likely to be an effect upon the levels of output, employment, and inflation, and upon the exchange rate of the country's currency.

The effect upon the level of demand, and hence national income, within the economy provides an important distinction between types of policies. Some will aim to raise or lower spending while others will aim to switch spending without changing income.

If a country has a deficit on its balance of payments, either approach might be used.

Expenditure-reducing policy

In terms of a country's circular flow of income, imports are a leakage from that flow and exports are an injection into it. This means that a change in the level of income will change the demand for imports, but not the demand for exports. If, therefore, the government can affect the level of income in the economy it will manage to change the balance of payments. Reducing the level of income will reduce import payments, without affecting export payments, and so reduce a deficit on the current account.

The government will have several ways in which it can reduce spending, and so, national income. Reductions in injections other than exports, or increases in leakages other than imports, will all achieve this result. Monetary and fiscal policy will provide the government with the weapons to do this.

The effects of expenditure-reducing policy on the level of national income, and the balance of payments, are shown in diagram 1. As income is reduced from Y1 to Y2, the payments deficit is cleared, by a fall in imports. The effects on output, and employ-

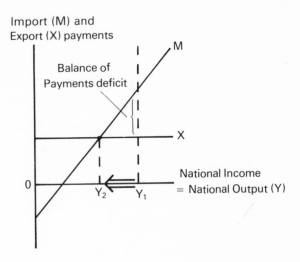

Reduced spending causes National Income to fall, so reducing import payments, until the Balance of Payments deficit is removed.

Diagram 1   Expenditure reducing

ment, may well be unpleasant, but equilibrium is restored to the balance of payments. This is achieved by a fall in the quantity rather than the price, of the products traded into the country.

Expenditure-switching policy

If consumers at home can be persuaded to spend less of their income on imports, and consumers abroad can be persuaded to spend more, then a payments deficit can be removed without changing the level of national income.

There are various ways in which the government might switch spending in this way. They might change the prices of particular products in trade, by imposing taxes and subsidies. They might change the prices of all products in trade, by changing the exchange rate of the country's currency. They might adjust the quantity of goods imported by imposing quotas.

Any of these measures will change the value of trade payments at each level of national income, as shown on diagram 2. As exports rise from X1 to X2, and imports fall from M1 to M2, the balance of payments deficit is cleared, and the level of national income remains unchanged. It may, however, be difficult to secure the approval of other countries for the changes in trading conditions that are necessary to achieve this result.

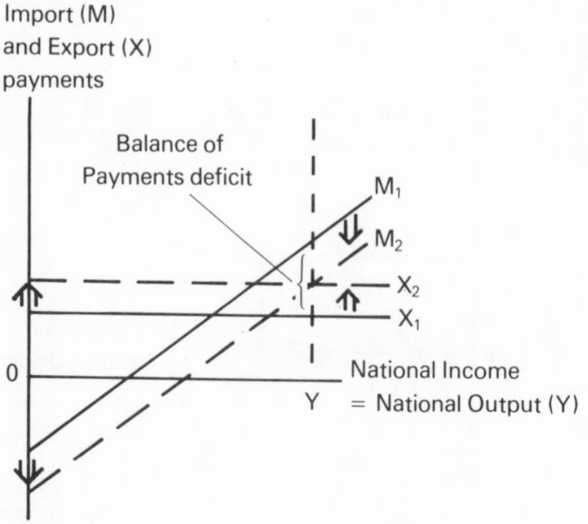

Import (M)
and Export (X)
payments

Expenditure is switched off imports on to exports, until the Balance of Payments deficit is removed, at the same level of National Income.

Diagram 2   Expenditure switching

'Why flagging exports could ruin the Government's Promised Land'

A run of bad trade figures puts increasing pressure on the government to introduce policies to correct the payments deficit. In our example here, such policies would be introduced well in advance of any significant strain on the reserves, and would be intended either to reduce or to switch expenditure.

In itself, a deficit of £179 million on payments from one month's trade need not be a matter of immediate concern to a country such as Britain. Indeed, this would seem to be confirmed by the fact that the balance, over a three-month period, was in slight surplus. It is in comparison with the earlier expectation of economists, however, that this figure becomes more significant and especially so at a time when Britain needed to repay large sums to other countries.

Faced with continuing deficits over a previous period, the British government had resorted to the temporary measure of borrowing from abroad. Other, more drastic policies had been applied in the meantime, and were by January expected to be leading the balance of payments into surplus. From that position of strength it was intended that the international loans should be repaid. In this context, the January figures were a serious disappointment. How should the government respond?

Why flagging exports could ruin the Government's Promised Land

The government's economic euphoria began to evaporate this week with news of a £179 million January trade gap. The figures baffled Whitehall, where officials searched in vain for excuses.

In the City, where some experts were forecasting a £145 million surplus, the pound was floored and shares slumped to their lowest for six months.

No wonder.

For the trade figures are among the most important numbers any Government has got to get right.

A run of bad trade figures does not immediately hit pay packets or the cost-of-living – but they are the reef on which the plans of many ambitious Chancellors have foundered.

They cannot be ignored without risking disastrous troubles for the pound.

They show whether we are paying our way in the world – or not.

If we spend more abroad on imports than we get for our exports we have to live on tick.

And in the last five years during which our Middle East oil bills quadrupled, we have run up a staggering £7,000 million of tick.

DEBTS

This year, our foreign creditors were hoping that, with North Sea oil flows near full spate, we would clear a big part of our long-overdue debts.

Money men were hoping that we could clock up an overall surplus of £2,000 million this year.

And that would mean we should be in the black on average by nearly £170 million each month.

The January figures mean that in the latest three months our trade was in the black by only a disappointing £111 million – compared to £720 million in the previous three months.

City economists are now cutting back their

Fewer tax cuts?

A reduction of £2000 million in the level of taxation would cause 'a spending spree', an increase in national income, and an increase in imports. If '25p in every £1 in our pay packets' were to be spent on imports, then a balance of payments deficit in January would become worse after the April Budget.

The need for expenditure-reducing policy is likely to convince the Chancellor that he should not allow these tax cuts. Austerity measures such as these are never popular. They bring a lower level of output and employment to the economy, which, in this case, will

estimates of a big surplus this year.

Many now fear it may be only £1,000 million – much less than our foreign creditors were hoping for.

This is bad news for families – because their hopes of a 4p in the £ rise in living standards are now fading.

These hopes were largely staked on a £2,000 million cut in taxes expected in the Chancellor's April Budget.

Now economists believe he cannot afford to unleash such a spending spree.

For an average of about 25p in every £1 in our pay packets would go on imported goods – and add to already-too-large import bills.

Without a corresponding rise in exports, a big fall in the value of the £ would follow – hoisting the price of imports in the shops, and adding to the cost-of-living.

But the threat to shoppers is not just to their purses – but to their freedom.

Soaring imports and a weak pound would step up the strong pressure on the Government for tough import clamps.

But they amount, in effect, to commanding the shopper to buy British goods, regardless of how shoddy or over-priced they are.

This would be sweeping under the carpet the real problem. To produce the right goods at the right price.

The latest figures show that exports plummeted by £150 million to £2,629 million last month.

RISES

This, according to City experts, reflects flagging output from British factories, coupled with big rises in the prices of British goods. . . .

Industry's competitiveness has been undermined by Stage Three pay rises greater than other industrial countries'.

And the 20 cent rise in the value of the £ which should have been a boon because it cut the price of imports for shoppers is now a millstone for industry.

Because factories cannot get their output to rise, the rise in the £ is added in full to our export prices.

Not surprisingly many of our customers are seeking cheaper supplies elsewhere.

Change the value of the pound?

The exchange rate of the pound, in terms of other countries' currencies, affects the selling prices of all goods traded by Britain. The '20% rise in the value of the pound' increased the relative prices of British goods and made them more difficult to sell at home and abroad. This 'millstone for industry' seems to have caused much of the difficulty in international trade. Products have been sold to other countries for higher prices, but in lower numbers, and the value of the payments earned from exports has fallen.

One expenditure-switching policy would be to lower the value of the pound, reverse this process, and improve the balance of payments without reducing national income.

QUESTIONS

(i)   Assume that the balance of payments is in equilibrium, when the government increases income by 4%. Show the effects on imports and exports on a diagram such as diagram 1.

(ii)   Explain how you would expect 'pay rises greater than in other industrial countries' to affect the British balance of payments.

(iii) How would 'living on tick' appear in the balance of payments accounts?

(iv)   Use the figures in the extract to calculate what the trade deficit would have been in January, if national income had been £2000 million greater at that time.

(v)   Which expenditure-reducing and expenditure-switching policies were introduced by Turkey to correct her payments deficit (see page 30)?

be 'bad news' for families whose hopes of 'a 4p in the £ rise in living standards are now fading'.

Import controls?

'Tough import clamps' would provide a drastic measure of expenditure-switching policy. The reduction in import payments that would follow, would improve the balance of payments situation, but at the cost of threatening relations with other countries and the 'freedom of the British shopper'. Neither would this policy improve exports directly – and this seemed to be the main concern in January.

8 International money

8.1 The market

When two countries trade there will be a flow of payments between them. If each country uses a different currency for its domestic transactions, these payments will be made in terms of both currencies. Exporters in one country will wish to be paid in their own currency, while importers in the other will wish to pay in theirs. There will need to be an exchange of currencies at some stage, in order to pay for the trade between them. The exchange rate will measure how much of one currency must be sold to buy more of the other.

International money

In many cases traders will be prepared to sell the currency of the importing country and buy the currency of the exporting country, in a direct exchange. Alternatively, they may choose a special type of currency to use as an intermediary, and make all of their payments between countries in terms of this international money.

There are not many currencies that will be suited to this type of work, for international money will be in demand only if it has earned the confidence of all traders.

It will, furthermore, be in supply only if it has been made available throughout the area of trade. Gold and the US dollar come closest to meeting these requirements.

Currency exchange

The exchange of one currency for another is generally achieved through free market forces. Whether a currency is in exchange directly for those of all other countries, or for international money alone, this exchange can be understood in terms of the interaction of supply and demand. Since there are many more than two countries involved in trade in the real world, the market is a complicated and far-reaching one. Traders themselves may find these complications off-putting, and will often make use of the specialist services of banks to advise them how to buy and sell,

Daily market report

The daily market report is input each morning and updated by the Latest Developments Report. It consists of:

> Several paragraphs on the early trends apparent in the London and European foreign exchange markets with most attention to the U.S. Dollar and Sterling.

> Factors behind currency movements are given as we see them. News items of major interest to the foreign exchange markets are often included.

> Second section gives spot rates for eight currencies (£/$, $/Dmk, $/French Franc, $/Commercial Belgian Franc, $/Swiss Franc, $/Dutch Guilder, $/Italian Lira, $/Japanese Yen). The London opening gold price is also included.

> Third section shows Euro deposit rates (1, 3, 6 and 12 month periods) for the Deutschemark, Swiss Franc, French Franc, Belgian Franc, Dutch Guilder and Euro Sterling, and the same periods plus three and five years for the Euro Dollar and domestic Sterling.

We obtain these rates from our dealers and from London brokers and they are indications of the state of the market and not prices upon which the bank will deal.

from day to day. We too can take some guidance on the nature of the market for currency exchange, from the banks who deal in it.

'Daily market report'

Supply and demand in the market are each influenced by many different things, for each individual currency. A bank will try to keep its clients informed about the changes that are happening in the market, and are expected to happen in the future. 'Uncertainties concerning the US economic outlook' and 'confusion over the trend in US interest rates' would both be expected to affect supply and demand for the dollar, relative to other currencies.

Exchange rates

The price of each currency is set by the interaction of demand and supply, and is expressed in terms of an exchange rate for other currencies. If, for example, one pound sterling can only be exchanged for a few dollars, its relative price is low. If it becomes worth more in terms of dollars, its relative price has risen.

30TH APRIL
MAJOR EUROPEAN CURRENCIES OPENED THIS MORNING LITTLE CHANGED FROM CLOSING LEVELS AGAINST THE U.S. DOLLAR. THE U.S. CURRENCY'S UNDERLYING WEAKNESS WAS STILL APPARENT HOWEVER AND DOLLAR WEAKENED FURTHER IN INITIAL TRADING AFTER YESTERDAY'S SHARP FALL. MAJOR FACTORS ATTRIBUTED TO THE FALL WERE UNCERTAINTIES CONCERNING THE U.S. ECONOMIC OUTLOOK, CONFUSION OVER THE TREND IN U.S. INTEREST RATES AND CONTINUING GERMAN BALANCE OF PAYMENTS SURPLUSES. WITH A 10 3/4 PERCENT PRIME RATE BECOMING COMMON AMONG U.S. COMMERCIAL BANKS, ROGER ANDERSON, CHAIRMAN OF CONTINENTAL ILLINOIS CORP. SUGGESTED IN LONDON YESTERDAY THAT PRIME RATES COULD BE EXPECTED TO REACH 11-12 PERCENT LEVEL BY THE SUMMER. THE FRENCH FRANC CONTINUED TO SLIDE ON EXCHANGE MARKETS YESTERDAY APPROACHING PSYCHOLOGICAL LEVEL OF ONE MARK TO 2 FRANCS. WEAKNESS SPURRED ON BY ALLEGATIONS BY FRANCOIS MITTERAND OF MISMANAGEMENT OF THE COUNTRY'S FINANCES BY GISCARD D'ESTAING. U.S. TREASURY BILLS WERE THREES 8.909 PC (7.857) AND SIXES 8.796 (7.995).

SPOT RATES (INDICATION ONLY)

POUND/DOLLAR	2.4405/15
DOLLAR/DMARK	2.4375/95
DOLLAR/FRFR	4.8425/75
DOLLAR/BFRC	37. 18/23
DOLLAR/SWFR	2.9065/95
DOLLAR/GUILDER	2.5700/25
DOLLAR/LIRA	632/633
DOLLAR YEN	279.30/70

GOLD DOLLARS 169/171 PREFIXING

EURO DEPOSIT RATES (INDICATION ONLY)

	EURO DOLLAR	DOMESTIC POUND
1M	11 9/16-7/16	13 3/8-1/8
3M	11 13/16-11/16	13 7/8-5/8
6M	11 9/16-7/16	14-13 3/4
1Y	10 5/8-1/2	14-13 3/4
3Y	10-9 3/4	14-13 3/4
5Y	10-9 3/4	13 3/4-3/8

	DMARK	SWFR
1M	8-7 3/4	6 3/4-1/2
3M	9-8 13/16	8 7/8-5/8
6M	9 1/2-5/16	9 3/4-1/2
1Y	9 1/2-1/4	9 5/8-3/8

Cash in one currency can be exchanged for cash in another at what is known as a 'spot rate'. The bank will inform its clients of the exchange rates of each major currency, in terms of dollars, and from these it would be possible to calculate the exchange rates between them. For example, if £1 is worth $2.4 (approximately) and $1 is worth 2.4 Marks (approximately), £1 must be worth (2.4 × 2.4 =) 5.76 Marks.

Money and loans

Money is anything that is generally acceptable in the settlement of debt. Within a country, its notes and coins are always immediately and generally acceptable in this way, but many other monetary assets are only slightly less acceptable. Loans can be for any length of time, and the shorter the period, the closer they are to becoming money.

So it is in the market for money at an international level. Purchasing power may be exchanged as 'spot' cash, or, in the postponed form of loans. The bank will inform its clients, therefore, of the prices of loans in each type of currency, as measured by the various rates of interest paid on different lengths of loans. Transactions in 'near-money' will then be made on a basis that is very similar to that for transactions in money itself.

QUESTIONS

(i)   Suggest one reason why the US dollar is more suitable as an international currency than the Swiss franc.

(ii)   Explain which types of international payments you would expect to be affected by the changes in interest rates in various countries.

(iii)   Which two changes are suggested in the extract that might affect the supply and demand for French francs?

(iv)   An investor could earn 14% from a year's deposit in terms of pounds, but only 9½% from a year's deposit in terms of German Deutschemark. How can interest rates be so much lower for Marks, and yet still attract investors?

8.2 Demand and supply

'Why the buck will stop here'

Why has the exchange rate of the dollar fallen '5% since the end of last month, and nearly 20% since the beginning of last year'? There are several possible reasons, for the USA has a 'basic payments deficit', and a need for companies to 'invest more in the

---

Why the buck will stop here

Is the market wrong about the dollar? Its weighted average exchange rate (against 20 currencies) has fallen 5% since the end of last month, and nearly 20% since the beginning of last year. A substantial fall in the dollar over that period was clearly necessary, because the $20bn a year basic payments deficit has been piling up more dollars abroad than foreigners want to hold. But is the rate now going too far, and over-adjusting? . . .

The inflation problem has figured in most of the analyses of what is wrong with the dollar. Yet if that were the main cause of its collapse, it is likely that the new prices and incomes policy (which, though controversial, is not entirely vacuous) would have steadied the dollar. Moreover, the US inflation rate, now about 8%, is less than that of the world as a whole.

Consequently, the dollar's decline has made US industry more competitive. Wholesale prices of manufactured goods in the US have fallen in relation to foreign competitors' export prices (in dollar terms) at about the same rate as the fall in the exchange rate. The dollar's fall has not been inflationary.

The fundamental problem is the current account deficit. The outlook here is for improvement, and Paul Armington, a former IMF official now with Wharton Economic Forecasting Associates, is optimistic.

"What is happening now is destabilising speculation," he says. "People are waiting for the current account to turn around. The trade balance in real terms has already turned around dramatically. Because of devaluation's effect on import prices, it will take a little longer to show improvement in cash terms. The dollar is now in a deep J-curve. But when the balance of payments turnaround is fully perceived, corporate treasurers will rebuild their dollar balances."

Companies will also invest more in the US. . . .

The US needs the gain in competitiveness to slash its current account deficit. Tough fiscal policy is the only other way and the outlook on that front is already stringent enough to foreshadow a mild recession in the US next year (what the Americans call a "growth recession"). . . .

To maintain competitiveness, however, the rising import prices due to the dollar's devaluation must not feed back heavily into domestic prices. This has not happened in the past in the US, to any great extent. But it could. That is why the counter-inflation programme was needed.

USA'. In addition there has been 'destabilising speculation' against the dollar.

The exchange rate of a currency is its relative price, set by market forces. The supply of, and demand for, a currency will follow from the payments that are made between countries since payments into a country involve a purchase of its currency, and payments out involve a sale. There are different types of demand and supply, just as there are different types of international payments, and each of the possible reasons for the dollar's decline is an example of one of these types.

Payments for the trade in products

When a trader wishes to import a good into the USA, he will need to exchange his dollars for the currency of the country he is importing from. Thus, imports into the USA involve a sale of US dollars. When a trader exports goods from the USA either he, or his purchaser, will need to exchange his payment of foreign currency into dollars. Thus, exports from the USA involve a purchase of US dollars.

If the USA is trading at a deficit, it is paying more for imports than it is being paid for exports. This will imply that more dollars are being sold than are being bought. In the market for dollars there is an excess of supply at the original price level, and the market clearing process will encourage a fall in the exchange rate of the dollar.

This is exactly the situation faced by the USA when 'the fundamental problem is the current account deficit'. The supply of dollars has been greater than the demand for them by $20 billion a year, and the 'deficit has been piling up more dollars abroad than foreigners want to hold'.

Payments of money capital

Whenever a loan is made from one country to another, it will, again, involve an exchange of currencies. Funds taken out of the USA and invested in some other country, will involve a sale of US dollars and a purchase of the country's currency. The returns on that loan will, however, result in payments into the USA at some future time (as the invisible earnings of a factor of production), and purchases of US dollars.

Companies have been unwilling to 'invest more in the US'. Some may have gone even further, and have preferred to transfer funds from the USA, and into other countries. This may have been due to differences in interest rates, or to differences in their expectations of future business prospects. In either case, it will have increased the supply of dollars to the international currency market, and encouraged a fall in the exchange rate.

Speculation

The exchange of countries' currencies is an area that is particularly suited to the skills of the speculator, and international currencies such as the dollar are especially vulnerable to his activities. Speculators can adjust their payments between countries in several ways, and so gain from changes in exchange rates.

Payments for trade in products can be made sooner or later in order to gain, or to avoid loss, from an expected fall in an exchange rate. Funds can be transferred from one country to another, and be lent on the very short-term, in order to gain from differences in interest rates, and expected changes in exchange rates. Currencies can be bought or sold in advance, on a 'futures' market, in order to gain from possible changes in exchange rates. In each of these cases, when the expectations of speculators coincide, they tend to become self-fulfilling.

Speculation against the dollar has been caused by the prospect of a fall in its exchange rate. That prospect is due less to the present basic deficit, than to the 'inflation problem' and the damage which that could do to the balance of payments in the future. As a result, speculators have advanced dollar payments, transferred funds from dollar accounts, and sold dollars, in advance, at the currently 'high' price. The result has been for more dollars to be sold in the currency markets, and for the exchange rate to fall. The speculators have proved themselves right.

Even so, this attack may be no more than the dollar deserves. Speculators' actions can have either a stabilising or a de-stabilising effect on a currency's price. At best, they will anticipate short-term changes in price perfectly, introducing them smoothly, and well in advance. At worst, they will exaggerate price fluctuations, and distort market forces, in the search for private gain.

In this example, it would appear that the dollar has suffered from 'de-stabilising speculation' and that its exchange rate has fallen rather too far.

Devaluation

All three of the main sources of demand and supply in the market for the dollar provide the same conclusion. There has been a greater supply, and a reduced demand for dollars in international markets, and price has fallen accordingly (see diagram 1). Since price is expressed as an exchange rate of the dollar for other currencies, this rate has been devalued.

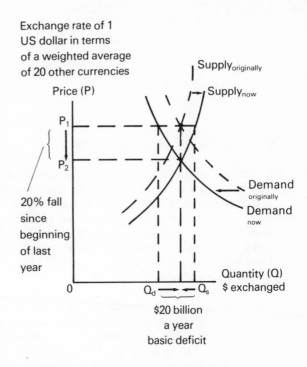

Diagram 1   A fall in the exchange rate of the dollar

QUESTIONS

(i)   From the information given, how would you expect the value of the US dollar to change in the month *following* its 5% fall? Explain this in terms of (a) payments for products, (b) payments of money capital, (c) speculation.

(ii)   What policies have been used to correct the USA's balance of payments deficit?

(iii)   Refer to 'the effect of oil payments on the UK', on page 29. How would you explain the fall in the exchange rate of the pound from 1 : $2.34 in 1974, to 1 : $2.20 in 1975, as a result of those payments alone?

9 Exchange rate policy

9.1 Official intervention

Currencies are generally exchanged for one another in a free international market, where price is set by supply and demand. The different types of payments that are made between countries give rise to different sources of trading in currencies. Supply and demand will follow from payments made for products and as loans between countries, and from speculation in the international exchange markets.

There is often one other type of trading in the market for a country's currency, and that is from the government of the country itself. Sometimes as an act of special policy, and sometimes as a matter of routine from day to day, there will be official intervention which is intended to influence the exchange rate set in the market.

The reasons for intervention

Stabilising speculation will anticipate changes in supply and demand with accuracy, and so ensure that price reflects the long-term conditions of the market. De-stabilising speculation will, however, exaggerate and distort any expected changes in price, so causing excessive fluctuations. The authorities might choose to intervene in order to balance these fluctuations, by setting their own activity against that of the speculators.

In addition, the authorities might wish to set the exchange rate at a level which is different from that implied by current market forces, for the effects that this might bring. Changes in the exchange rate will affect the balance of payments and the domestic economy of a country in ways that will concern the government, and which are studied later.

Fixed and flexible exchange rates

The authorities must choose how much to intervene and in what way. If they intervene a very great deal they may be able to keep the exchange rate at a predetermined level. If price is to stay *fixed*, however, they will need to balance every change in demand or supply with an opposite adjustment of their own.

At the other extreme, they may choose not to intervene at all, and allow the exchange rate to be completely *flexible*, and set only by the types of demand and supply that follow from trade and capital payments. Most often they will maintain some measure of control, but alter the pattern of their intervention from time to time.

Methods of intervention

If the international market for a country's currency is a free one, intervention will only be possible through the forces of supply and demand. Either the authorities will need to alter the value of payments for trade and as capital, or they will need to buy or sell on their own part. It is the second, and more direct form of intervention that will be considered here.

'The pound holds steady up to June'

In the period until April, Britain saw 'five months of large-scale inflows' on its balance of payments. As a result the demand for pounds tended to exceed supply in the international currency markets. This encouraged a rise in the pound's exchange rate from its original level of £1 : $1.72, a rise which, for various reasons, the authorities wished to prevent.

Their policy was, therefore, to meet the excess demand for pounds from their own supply. Since the authorities are responsible for issuing their own country's currency, there is no difficulty in finding

---

The pound holds steady up to June

Official policy on the exchange rate, now that money has started to flow out of Britain after five months of large-scale inflows, is to use the foreign currency that was taken into the reserves between December and April to hold the rate at its present $1.71 to $1.72 level. Whitehall officials stress that the Chancellor's warning to the unions yesterday that another wage explosion would "send the pound plummeting" does not in any way mean that he is about to pull the rug from under the pound, or deliberately lower the official intervention rate.

The pound is now strong in some ways, and potentially weak in others. The basic balance of payments is not in deficit, and moreover the reserves — just below $10 billion now — are $4.8 billion higher than at the end of November. Its potential weakness lies in the very low margin of interest rates above

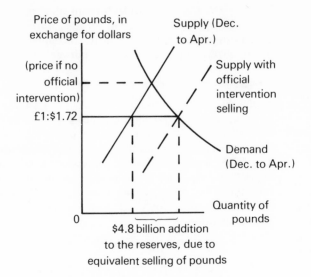

Diagram 1   Intervention selling of pounds

pounds to sell in this way. Their exchange of pounds for foreign currency matched supply to demand at the £1 : $1.72 level, as shown in diagram 1.

The effect of this policy upon the official reserves was as follows. The payments surplus in itself was bringing extra foreign earnings into the country. The intervention selling of pounds, and buying of foreign currency, absorbed all of those extra payments into the reserves. No wonder they rose by $4.8 billion to their 'current' level of 'just below $10 billion'.

those on dollar deposits, and the high rate of inflation.

Last month was the first since November in which the Bank of England had to intervene to stop the pound from falling. After allowing for foreign currency borrowing by the Government, the Bank's currency reserves fell by $605m. Officials regard this mainly as the result of the unusually low difference in interest rates between dollar and sterling deposits. This gap has shrunk to about 2%, compared with a normal 3.5% to 4% in recent years — and a high of nearly 10% last November.

The present policy of using the reserves build-up between December and April to hold the existing rate means that if sterling is sold, due to the narrow interest differential or because of speculation, the authorities will support the pound using the influx of "effervescent flows" that were taken into the reserves during those months. These are estimated at about $4,250m — of which about $600m flowed out last month.

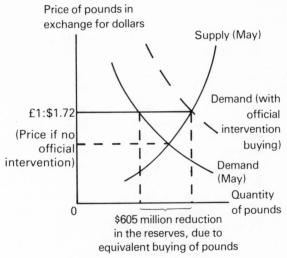

Diagram 2   Intervention buying of pounds

May and June

The flow of short-term capital that had been paid into Britain in previous months, began to be paid out again in the period after April. An estimated $4250 million had been paid in, but 'about $600 million flowed out' in May alone.

This reversed the pressure on the pound and brought supply up to exceed demand. To prevent a fall in the exchange rate, the authorities sold $605 million of foreign currency from their reserves in May and bought pounds on the international market. The effect was to maintain the exchange rate at its previous level, of £1 : $1.72, as shown in diagram 2.

QUESTIONS

(i)   What is meant in the extract by the 'basic' balance of payments?

(ii)   Use the figures given for the change in the reserves, and the 'effervescent flows' of capital, to estimate the value of that basic balance from December to April.

(iii)   Suggest two ways, *other* than direct intervention, in which the authorities might have kept the exchange rate of the pound constant from December to April.

(iv)   Refer to page 26, 'Nice timing by Treasury'. Draw a supply and demand diagram to illustrate the effect of intervention by the German Bundesbank upon the market, and the exchange rate of the Deutschemark, in November.

9.2 The terms of trade

A country's *terms of trade* relate the prices of the goods it exports to the prices of the goods it imports.

$$\text{(The terms of trade} = \frac{\text{A weighted index of all export prices}}{\text{A weighted index of all import prices}}\text{)}$$

This relationship is clearly an important one, since it influences the trading process, the gains from trade, and the payments made for trade. It will also decide the impact of exchange rate changes.

A country's terms of trade can change because of a change in export prices, a change in import prices, or both. Inflation inside a country will raise its export prices, and inflation in the rest of the world will raise its import prices. Different rates of inflation between the home country and the rest of the world will cause the terms of trade to change.

A change in the relative prices of different goods will also affect the terms of trade if the country exports and imports different types of goods. If there is a fall in the prices of the types of goods it exports, or a rise in the prices of the types of goods it imports, then the terms of trade will fall.

Finally, a change in a country's exchange rate will affect the relative prices of its exports and imports. Export prices will change in terms of foreign currency, and import prices will change in terms of the country's own currency. If the exchange rate rises, home currency is worth less in terms of foreign currency; home goods become relatively more expensive than foreign goods, and the terms of trade rise. If the exchange rate falls, then so also will the terms of trade.

Is a change in the terms of trade 'good' or 'bad'?

A rise in a country's terms of trade will affect it in two ways. On the one hand it will be able to exchange more foreign goods for the same quantity of its own goods. For the present, this will allow the country to capture more of the gains from trade, and will raise its income in real terms. This will be welcomed.

On the other hand, the country will find it more difficult to sell its own products from now on. At their relatively higher price, its own products are less competitive in world markets, and against imports in its home market. The country will appear to have lost some degree of cost advantage in world trade, and will sell, to some extent, fewer of its own products. This will not be welcomed.

Since one country's exports are always another's

imports, a rise in one country's terms of trade must always be matched by a fall in those of other countries. Both parties in trade will suffer 'mixed blessings' from a change in the terms of trade between them.

'Trade terms "harder for Japan" '

A change in the terms of trade against Japan and other manufacturing countries, seems to have been caused by an equal change in favour of the countries that export oil. This has increased the share of the gains from trade going to the oil producers, but has made them less competitive in world trade. In their case, this is scarcely of concern, since they specialise in exporting goods for which there can be no effective competition.

> # Trade terms 'harder for Japan'
>
> The terms of trade have moved more sharply against Japan in recent years than against either the U.S. or the EEC according to new statistics collected by the United Nations Conference on Trade and Development (UNCTAD).
>
> The UNCTAD secretariat offers no explanation for the phenomenon, although the reason would seem to be a combination of the severer impact on Japan — which imports virtually all its fuel — of the increase in oil prices and Japan's success in holding down the prices of its exports. . . .
>
> By contrast major oil exporters had registered a threefold improvement in their terms of trade. Other developing countries suffered a decline similar to the U.S. and Europe — though there has probably been a further worsening in their terms of trade since then with the downward trend in primary commodity prices.

QUESTIONS

(i)   State two causes of changes in the terms of trade between countries that are mentioned in the extract.

(ii)   Why should 'holding down the price of its exports' be a success from Japan's point of view?

(iii)   Why did some developing countries gain, and some lose, from the change in the terms of world trade?

The terms of trade and the balance of payments

A change in the relative prices of the goods that a country sells to, and buys from foreign countries, is almost certain to affect its own balance of payments. Even if the amount of trade were to remain the same, goods traded at different prices would require different payments. In fact, the amount of trade will be affected as well, and payments will be changed in two different ways.

A fall in a country's export prices, for example, will reduce the payments that are received for the same quantity of goods. However, the fall in prices is also likely to encourage foreigners to buy a greater quantity of those goods, and so tend to increase the payments received from them. As a result, payments for exports might fall, rise, or stay the same, depending on how much demand responds to the price change.

'Europe likes a cut'

A fall in the price of British exports seems to have a different effect upon the quantity demanded of them, in different countries. A 1% fall in the relative prices of British exports seems to increase the volume of goods sold to the EEC by 1.35%, but to the USA by 0.80%. This difference is of critical importance to the balance of payments.

A 1% fall in prices will reduce payments for the same quantity of exports by 1%. A 1.35% rise in quantity will increase payments by 1.35%. The British balance of payments with the EEC will improve, following a reduction in British export prices. This is in contrast to the situation in the USA, where, on the same basis, payments for British exports would decrease.

Price elasticity of demand

A change in a country's terms of trade shows that the relative prices of its exports and imports have changed. Those changes can affect the flow of payments for exports and imports one way or the other. The overall effect on the balance of payments will depend upon how much demand responds to the price changes. This is measured by the price elasticity of demand (PED) for exports and imports, where the PED is found from the formula:

$$PED = \frac{\% \text{ change in quantity demanded}}{\% \text{ change in price}}$$

If both export and import prices change in relation to their competition, their combined PEDs will determine the effect upon the balance of payments. A fall in the terms of trade will improve the balance of payments if combined PEDs add up to more than one, but worsen it if they are less than one.

Europe likes a cut

For British exporters, price-cutting works best in the Common Market. In fact, it boosts the volume of sales there at least 1½ times as much as in America or in the less-developed Commonwealth countries.

These are among the conclusions which emerge from a new study of British exports by a group of Cambridge economists working with Professor Richard Stone's complex economic growth model. It will be published this summer by Chapman Hall in Economic Structure and Policy, edited by Terence Barker.

The Common Market, of all Britain's major export markets, is easily the most sensitive to price changes. This finding is important because a steadily increasing portion of UK exports goes to the EEC, due to tariff cuts. Tariff barriers will be removed completely in just more than a year's time.

This should make devaluations of sterling more effective than in the past — assuming the Common Market continues to take an increasing share of our exports.

For every 1% fall in British prices compared with foreign ones, export volume to the EEC rises 1.35%; to the USA 0.80%, to the less-developed Commonwealth countries 0.85%; and to the former white Commonwealth countries 1.1%.

These figures do not reflect differences between broad categories of goods shipped to the different markets, because the Cambridge group adjusted for this factor.

Looking at export markets on a global basis, high technology and capital goods products are fairly insensitive to price, the study shows. The most price-sensitive product category is travel goods, clothing and footwear, followed by textiles. For these, gains in export volume tend to be between two and three times the price cut (both expressed as percentages).

QUESTIONS

(i)   What would be the effect for Britain of a rise in the exchange rate of the pound upon the payments earned from exports to each of the following areas:
(a) the EEC;
(b) the USA;
(c) less-developed Commonwealth;
(d) former white Commonwealth?
(ii)   Suggest two types of products to specialise in, if Britain wished to raise her exchange rate and export earnings.
(iii)   According to the figures given, what is the PED for exports (a) to the EEC, (b) to the USA, (c) of travel goods, clothing, etc. . . . ?
(iv)   Under what circumstances (i.e. what value of PEDs) will a rise in the terms of trade (a) improve, (b) worsen the balance of payments?

9.3 The effects of exchange rate changes

'A strong pound that may prove a weak link'

A change in the exchange rate of the pound has a widespread effect upon the British economy. It affects the trading position of British firms in foreign and home markets. It affects the flow of payments in and out of the country. It affects the levels of output, jobs and prices in the domestic economy. Each of these is a matter of concern to the government, and will decide them on the policy they should apply in the currency exchange markets.

Trade

A rise in the relative price of the pound will, other things being equal, raise the terms of trade facing Britain. Exports will appear more expensive, imports will appear less expensive, and Britain will lose some measure of any advantage it had in trade.

As a result, British consumers will be 'better off' in terms of foreign goods and services, as holiday-makers will find from their 'unexpected bonus'. British products, however, will be less competitive in comparison with those from other countries — as ICI has found at a cost of 'nearly £70 million in lost sales'. The pattern of international trade, and the distribution of gains from it, between Britain and other countries, will both have been affected by this rise in the exchange rate of the pound.

The balance of payments

A rise in the terms of trade will affect the balance of payments in a way that depends upon price elasticities of demand (PED). It seems probable that the combined PEDs for British exports and imports add up to more than one, so that a change in relative prices will bring a more than proportionate change in quantity. This effect may take some months to get under way, but it will then lead to a worsening of the balance of payments. Indeed it would appear that, in our example, this damage has

---

A strong pound that may prove a weak link

For anyone about to go on holiday the dizzy rise of the pound on the foreign exchange markets will come as an unexpected bonus. A pound today buys almost 3 per cent more dollars than it did a week ago and almost 20 per cent more than July last year.

The problem arises not in going on holiday but in coming back. The main casualty of a soaring pound is British industry, which is watching the foreign exchange markets with increasing anxiety; hundreds of thousands of jobs could eventually hang on the outcome.

A strong pound makes exports — already difficult to come by — more expensive and imports proportionately cheaper. Manufacturing companies are thus doubly hit. They find it more difficult to sell abroad while cheaper imports flood into the country displacing goods which otherwise would have been supplied by domestic companies.

The erosion of export competitiveness is partly compensated by the fact that imported raw materials and components are cheaper, though this takes some time to filter through the manufacturing process. . . .

This situation is not new for Britain. As long ago as April last year — when sterling was "only" 1.93 against the dollar — ICI, our biggest company, warned that it was 10 per cent overvalued. Since then the company has become more agnostic, believing that industry must live with whatever sterling rate the foreign exchange markets dictate. But ICI does not

deny that the strength of sterling reduces export competitiveness, and it admits that last year's appreciation of the pound cost it nearly £70 millions in lost sales.
. . .

The problem is particularly serious for Britain for two reasons:

First, we were not particularly successful at exporting, even when a lower pound made our goods cheaper. The main industrial problem in Britain over the last decade has been that imports of manufactured goods have continually risen far faster than exports, creating a balance of payments problem so great that even North Sea oil is not able to shield us from the consequences.

This can be seen from the Treasury's Budget forecasts which indicate that the balance of payments will barely be in surplus in the first half of next year, notwithstanding the fact the country by then will be totally self-sufficient in oil. The situation may be worse if the experience of the first five months of this year is anything to go by. In the January-May period the balance of payments was more than £1 billion in deficit as imports swilled into the country. These can hardly be described as text-book conditions for a policy which hinders exports and facilitates imports.

Second, the reason for sterling's strength has nothing to do with the industrial situation in Britain. It is strong solely because Britain discovered large quantities of oil and, in the wake of the latest OPEC oil price rises, the pound has become a "petro-currency" and bankers are caught in a Gadarene rush to buy as much of it as they can.

already been done, since in 'the January — May period the balance of payments was more than £1 billion in deficit as imports swilled into the country'.

There are other conditions that may have influenced this result, besides changes in the demand for imports and exports. The terms of trade are set by more than the exchange rate alone, and may also have been affected by relative rates of price inflation, or the relative prices of different types of goods traded.

Furthermore, the response of different countries to the changed conditions in trade will not always be the same, and suppliers in Britain may generally be less adaptable than those in other countries. Differences in supply, such as this, might explain why British suppliers 'were not particularly successful at exporting even when a lower pound made our goods cheaper'.

Finally, it must be remembered that the balance of payments reflects exchanges of money capital as well as products. The Investments section of the accounts is unlikely to be affected in a direct way by changes in the relative prices of products, but a change in the real return from international investments will follow from a change in the exchange rate. As a result, investors of short-term funds may well respond to the attraction of a strong pound and be caught in 'a Gadarene rush to buy as much of it as they can'.

The economy

'Hundreds of thousands of jobs could eventually hang on the outcome' of changes in the foreign exchange markets. Changes in the flow of payments in and out of the economy will affect the levels of injections and leakages in the circular flow of income. If income falls, then there will be pressure for real output, employment and prices, all to decrease.

If the economy was previously at a level of output that gave full employment, but no inflation, the reduction in demand will cause a deflationary gap, and unemployment (see diagram 1).

If there was inflation previously, there is likely to be a change in its level as well. Inflation from demand sources will be reduced, as the balance of payments moves into deficit. Inflation from supply sources will be reduced, by the falling cost of imported raw materials and components.

Policy

All of these effects of a rise in the exchange rate are clearly of concern to the government, and suggest that such changes should be controlled. Techniques are available for both indirect or direct intervention in the currency markets, and yet, the opportunities for consistent and enduring policies are limited.

The government can maintain a high exchange rate directly, only as long as it has the reserves to support its intervention. It can maintain a low exchange rate only as long as there remains the political will to accept decreased living standards.

In practice, it will not be possible for any government to maintain the exchange rate of its currency at an 'unrealistic' level, for any length of time, without extensive support from others. Since one country's gain is usually another's loss, that support is not lightly given.

QUESTIONS

(i)   Briefly explain the effect of a rising pound upon the balance of payments (a) in the short-term before the quantity of trade begins to change, (b) in the long-term.

(ii)   Briefly explain the effect of a balance of payments deficit upon the value of the pound.

(iii)   Why has the pound's exchange rate risen here? Answer in terms of *all* the main sources of supply and demand for pounds.

(iv)   Under what conditions will a rise in the exchange rate *not* change the terms of trade?

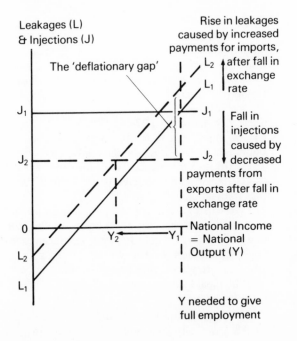

Diagram 1   The effects of a strong pound on the economy

Suggested answers

2.2 Britain and Japan
(i) (b). (ii) (a). (iii) (a). (iv) (b). (v) (a).

3.1 Bid to buy British
(i) Indian rugs/Kenyan coffee. (ii) Most goods from Japan/USA/Europe, etc. (iii) Floppy cricket hats. (iv) Norwegian salesgirls.

3.2 Oats or barley
(i) A: $\frac{1}{2}$ for oats, $\frac{4}{7}$ for barley; B: $\frac{4}{5}$ for oats; $\frac{2}{3}$ for barley. (ii) Yes; A barley: B oats. (iii) Diagram 1. (iv) Exchange or alter, land/labour/capital/enterprise. *Lancashire cotton* (i) The training and skills of labour, and the quality of machines. (ii) Labour working harder in Japan, technical progress. (iii) Factor transfers, more machinery in Japan, etc.

Oats (tons/acre)

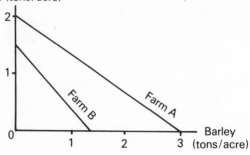

Diagram 1

3.3 Trade in potatoes
(i) £27 a ton (if no trading costs). (ii) Diagram 1, section 3.3, applied to chips, with Britain as market B. (iii) Diagram 2, section 3.3, applied to Holland, with chips as good Y, and potatoes as good X. (iv) Official price set below equilibrium price. Excess demand attracted illegal imports.

4.1 Free trade
(i) $1\frac{1}{16}$ of wine for $1\frac{1}{10}$ of cloth. (ii) +75 tons of oats, −25 tons of barley. (iii) 125 tons of oats for 150 tons of barley. (iv) Risk from disease, weather, etc; costs in changing production, etc.

4.2 Best of British
(i) (a) Imperfections; (b) specialisation, income distribution. (ii) In Britain, through prices; in Russia, by law. (iii) Russian are nearly all primary; British are nearly all tertiary. (iv) Russia has advantages in land, Britain in skilled labour and capital. (v) Losses from risk of specialising, from cost in adapting production, or in distribution of gains.

4.3 Time for the chop
(i) (a) Imperfections, infant industry; (b) unemployment, strategic industry, relative gain. (ii) (a) Infant industry, unemployment; (b) others. (iii) No, yes, either. (iv) (a) Import quota; (b) government subsidy. (v) Loss of comparative advantage will lead to low output, unemployment, and eventual bankruptcy.

5.1 Exporting rail
(i) In (a). (ii) Out (c). (iii) In (a). (iv) In (b). (v) In (a). (vi) In (b). (vii) Out (c).

5.2 New Zealand
(i) Production of butter, national income and employment all rise. (ii) Fewer gains from comparative advantage, higher food prices, lost export earnings from New Zealand, and lost returns on £500 million investment. (iii) A subsidy to Irish producers, a tariff, a quota on New Zealand imports. (iv) Wool production (a complement to sheepmeat) is cut, so price rises.

6.1 Nice timing by Treasury
(i) Dollars, special drawing rights. (ii) A fall of $50 million only, because less foreign currency taken from the reserves. (iii) (a) Rise; (b) kept down. (iv) Reserves rise in October, but fall later when loan repaid with interest.

6.2 The Accounts, 1974 and 1975
(i) An improvement in the large deficit on visible trade, but a reversal of the large inflow of capital, in 1975. (ii) (a) Visible exports; (b) invisible exports; (c) capital outflow (export credit); (d) official financing (net transactions with IMF).
The Oil Crisis (i) and (ii) UK pays less for oil, due to slump; UK sells more visible exports, as OPEC spends more of income on consumption; UK receives less in loans, as inflation, exchange rate, interest rates make UK less attractive. (iii) Prefer current, since loans must be repaid with interest.

7.1 When the reserves run out!
(i) All years. (ii) $6.9 billion (=1.9 last year, 1.0 in loans to be repaid, 4.0 in current account deficit). (iii) Output and employment both reduced.

7.2 Flagging exports
(i) Diagram 1, section 7.2, but income rises from Y2 to Y1, causing a payments deficit. (ii) At first, an ·improvement; later a deficit is likely, due to lost competitiveness. (iii) A capital account surplus to balance a current account deficit. (iv) (£179 m + (£2000m/12 × 25p/100p) =) £221 million approx. (v) Austerity measures, devaluation.

8.1 Daily market report
(i) Swiss francs are not available throughout the world, as dollars are. (ii) Short-term flows of money capital. (iii) 'Psychological level', 'financial mis-management'. (iv) if Germany has a stronger exchange rate, and lower inflation.

8.2 Why the buck will stop here
(i) (a), (b), (c) all expected to increase the demand for dollars in future. (ii) Fiscal restraint, prices and incomes, devaluation. (iii) Moved into payments deficit, so less demand for pounds.

9.1 The pound holds steady
(i) Balance on current and long-term capital payments. (ii) Reserves rose by (4.8 + 0.605 =) $5.4 billion. Effervescent flows were (4.250 + .600 =) $4.850 billion. Therefore, basic balance was (5.4 − 4.85 =) $555 million. (iii) Lower interest rates, increased loan repayments by the government. (iv) Diagram 1, section 9.1, applied to Deutschemark.

9.2 Trade terms 'Harder for Japan'
(i) Rise in oil prices, Japan holding down export prices, fall in commodity prices. (ii) More competitive export prices, so balance of payments and growth will improve in future. (iii) Oil exporters gained, others lost.
Europe likes a cut (i) (a) Fall; (b) rise; (c) rise; (d) fall. (ii) High technology and capital goods products. (iii) (a) 1.35; (b) 0.8 (c) 2 or 3. (iv) Combined PEDs for exports and imports (a) less than one; (b) greater than one.

9.3 A strong pound
(i) (a) Improves before elasticities operate; (b) worsens as elasticities (if greater than one) operate. (ii) Excess supply of pounds, so exchange rate falls. (iii) 'Basic' balance is 'barely in surplus', short-term flow of capital is in strong surplus, authorities have not intervened to prevent the excess demand for pounds causing a rise in exchange rate. (iv) If changes in inflation rates, or in relative prices of goods traded, cancel out the effect of exchange rate changes.

Sources

8.2 'Why the Buck Will Stop Here'
Crawford, M., *The Sunday Times* 29.10.78

9.1 'The Pound Holds Steady up to June'
Crawford, M., *The Sunday Times* 5.6.77

9.2 'Trade Terms "Harder for Japan"'
Housego, D., *The Financial Times* 8.6.78

'Europe Likes a Cut'
Barker, T. (ed.), *Economic Structure and Policy* (Chapman Hall) 1976

9.3 'A Strong Pound that May Prove a Weak Link'
Keegan, V., *The Guardian* 5.7.79

2.2 'What Britain and Japan Sell to Each Other'
Japan Information Centre, Embassy of Japan, *British Trade with Japan* January 1977, p. 1

3.1 'One Man's Bid to Buy British'
Ellsworth-Jones, W., *The Sunday Times* 21.5.78

3.2 'Oats or Barley?'
Norman, L. and Coote, R. B., *The Farm Business* (Longman) 1971, pp. 101-103

'Lancashire Cotton'
Bowker, B., *Lancashire under the Hammer* (L. & V. Woolf) 1928, p. 23

3.3 'Trade in Potatoes'
Rose, G., *The Sunday Times* 30.4.78

4.1 'Possible Gains from Comparative Advantage'
Ricardo, D., *The Principles of Political Economy and Taxation* (J. M. Dent & Sons) 1926 (originally published 1817) pp. 82-3

'Free Trade'
Tooke, Thomas, *The 1820 Petition of the London Merchants* quoted in McCord, N., *Free Trade* (David & Charles) 1970 p. 49

4.2 'The Best of British'
Leslie, A. *Daily Mail* 12.10.78

4.3 'Time for the Chop'
Mirror Comment, *Daily Mirror* 10.2.78

5.1 'Exporting Rail'
Harris, M., *The Times* 12.5.78

5.2 'New Zealand'
The Times 13.6.78

6.1 'Nice Timing by Treasury'
The Daily Telegraph 3.11.78

7.1 'When the Reserves Run Out!'
Munir, M., *The Financial Times* 2.3.78

7.2 'Why Flagging Exports Could Ruin the Government's Promised Land' Fingleton, E., *Sun* 17.2.78

8.1 'Daily Market Report'
International Marine Banking Co. Ltd., *Intermarine* 1974

Index